The voice of educators and education students

Mike Watts, Yujuan Luo, Tawinan Saengkhattiya, Lisa Arthur Bonful, Wu Yu, Ling Li, Najma Fazal and Hodan Ahmed

Department of Education, Brunel University London

With contributions from

Cathy Gower, Benjamin Zephaniah, Phil Renshaw, Jenny Robinson, Mike Watts, Yujuan Luo, Nic Crowe, Gail Waite, Philip Garner, Christopher Ince, Kate Hoskins, Lewis Fogarty, Antoine J Rogers, Wendy King, Balbir Kaur, Asgar Halim Rajput, Najwa Iggoute, Jin Jiang, Pauline Sithole, Tawinan Saengkhattiya, Rachel Milburn, Shane De Fonseka, Ling Li, Yu Wu, Anita Sediqi, Zahrah Mahmood, Bhavisha Soma, Joseph Hanley, Rich Barnard, Sichen Chen, Abdirazak Osman, Jawaher Almutairi, Priya Jaswal, Carolina Akinyi Nyakila, Monia Al-Farsi, Mohamad Adning and Lisa Arthur Bonful

The voice of educators and education students

The Department of Education
Brunel University London

© All rights reserved

The Copyright of each contribution rests with the individual authors, unless otherwise specified, and no part of this publication may be reproduced, stored in a retrieval system or transmitted in any form or by any means without the prior written permission of the individual authors or contributors.

ISBN: 9798666712696

Foreword

Dr Cathy Gower

Well, I wondered when Professor Mike Watts and our doctoral researcher Yujuan (Sophia) Luo announced that we would be doing a second Department of Education anthology whether it would be at all possible to reach the dizzy heights of our first edition. I had nothing to worry about. Indeed, what appears to have happened is an even wider range of contributions from staff, students at all levels, doctoral researchers and some special guest appearances too. This is something to be incredibly proud of and showcases the energy, passion and humour of our collective. Once again, we have the most amazingly diverse range of writing represented here. There is poetry, reflective pieces, diary entries, research-related summaries, discussion pieces, conversational extracts, provocations, advocacy, reminiscence and some contributions which I could not and should not attempt to pigeon hole in any way. It is truly a celebration of the wonderful community that is the Department of Education at Brunel University London. I want to extend my thanks to all who have taken time to think and write and we hope our readers enjoy the shared experience. Finally, a special thanks to our editorial team, led by the wonderful Sophia, and Mike for his continued enthusiasm for and commitment to this special series.

CONTENTS

1   **Why Noor didn't want to get on the trampoline**
      Cathy Gower

12   **Civil Lies and For Word**
      Benjamin Zephaniah

16   **ON BEING DONALD TRUMP: How gamification helps research philosophy make sense. [OR] the surprising link to your research philosophy**
      Phil Renshaw   Jenny Robinson

25   **Should we be educating for activism?**
      Mike Watts

32   **What should we expect of online learning and teaching under the background of the Coronavirus outbreak?**
      Yujuan Luo

41   **The perfect girl is gone**
      Nic Crowe

51   **Stories of 'shame': how can Nathanson's compass of shame help us understand problematic behaviour?**
      Gail Waite

60   **Circling the Cairo cement works and dented Dodges: a tale of daring and survival**
      Philip Garner

66	**Quack: a reflection on teaching science in a UK secondary school** *Christopher Ince*	
71	**Theorising 'success'** *Kate Hoskins*	
80	**Advocating for education and care in equal measure throughout education** *Lewis Fogarty*	
87	**A diasporic response to Black Lives Matter** *Antoine J Rogers*	
93	**Conversations with students** *Wendy King*	
99	**The yellow brick road** *Balbir Kaur*	
109	**A mature student's experience of higher education** *Asgar Halim Rajput*	
116	**Struggles of a mother and teacher: swimming against the tide** *Najwa Iggoute*	
121	**Why do I always want to be a teacher?** *Jin Jiang*	
128	**A daring adventure** *Pauline Sithole*	
136	**Curiosity - the magic wink in children's eyes: an observation story by me** *Tawinan Saengkhattiya*	
143	**A new dawn** *Rachel Milburn*	
146	**Beware the demon in the well: (Ancient) Sri Lankan superstitions, and their modern day explanations** *Shane De Fonseka*	

153	**Training centre experiences**
	Ling Li
160	**Some personal insights in my teaching experience: what do children think of their parents?**
	Yu Wu
165	**My journey of life**
	Anita Sediqi
168	**It's (not) fine**
	Zahrah Mahmood
172	**What a world it could be!**
	Bhavisha Soma
178	**The negative impact of student evaluations on higher education research**
	Joseph Hanley
185	**QTS professional skills tests: to pass, or too passé**
	Rich Barnard
194	**What is the point of cognitive academic language learning approach (CALLA)?**
	Sichen Chen
199	**Vocational education and training (VET): skills training or individual formation?**
	Abdirazak Osman
207	**Intercultural perspectives in multicultural education**
	Jawaher Almutairi
212	**Class and educational achievement**
	Priya Jaswal
221	**Is the government doing enough to promote good oral health in children?**
	Carolina Akinyi Nyakila
230	**Can e-learning make them skillful?**
	Monia Al-Farsi

236 **Can the augmented reality and virtual reality be applied in the open university?**
Mohamad Adning

244 **Online student tutoring from a tutor's perspective**
Lisa Arthur Bonful

The voice of educators and education students

Cathy Gower

I am privileged to be the Head of the Department of Education in the College of Business Arts and Social Sciences (CBASS). I joined Brunel University in 1997 as the coordinator for the PGCE Secondary Physical Education with QTS programme and also worked extensively on both the BSc Secondary Physical Education with QTS programme and the BA Secondary Physical Education programme. My work on these programmes was informed by my career up to that point as a teacher of Physical Education and English in two local London boroughs. I went on to become the Deputy Head of Teaching and Learning and then Director of Initial Teacher Education in the Department and worked with an amazing team of ITE colleagues and students to secure an outstanding judgement from Ofsted at our last inspection for both primary and secondary provision. I am particularly proud to be the Head of the Department of Education at Brunel University London having previously been an undergraduate, masters and doctoral student at the University myself. I am passionate about how our work as staff and students can contribute significantly to the advancement of research and practice in relation to both the education of young people and the education of practitioners in a range of different educational settings.

The voice of educators and education students

Why Noor didn't want to get on the trampoline

Cathy Gower

I sat down with my student PGCE PE teacher, Jane, to watch captured video footage of her self-selected year 9, mixed-sex trampolining lesson in a predominantly Asian Muslim secondary school in West London. I had noticed (and I will come back to this term later) a female pupil, Noor, who had adopted the most ingenious avoidance strategy. As she anticipated her turn to get on, she subtly manoeuvred herself around the edge of trampoline so that, on each occasion, she missed her turn. As the pupils chattered away 'spotting' for each other, they were completely oblivious to her artful tactics. Time and time again, she shuffled round the person next to her, placed her hands on the blue surround matting to demonstrate she was paying due care and attention to her fellow pupils' safety and engaged in the pupil 'banter' as they took their turns to complete the five-bounce routine. Eventually, I pressed pause on the laptop and said, "Jane, have you noticed Noor has not got on the trampoline for the whole lesson?"

So why did Noor not want to get on the trampoline? Why had Jane not noticed her avoidance tactics while she taught the lesson or indeed now as we watched the footage? Why had I noticed Noor?

Of what significance is any of this? I will get to these questions but, initially, I will provide a bit of context.

Jane and I were experimenting with an alternative pedagogical approach to lesson observation in Initial Teacher Education (ITE) as part of a research project I was conducting. This project sought to disrupt the traditional power hierarchies in lesson observation processes, where the visiting university ITE tutor or mentor has 'seen' the lesson in advance in real time and is, therefore, in a privileged position to ask questions about the observed practice and the student teacher is normally trying to second guess the 'right' answer they think the tutor or mentor wants to hear. The voice of the student teacher is usually subjugated and, invariably, the whole scenario ends up being a highly pressurised and discomforting situation for them. On too many occasions student teachers become overwhelmed by what they perceive to be a high-stakes, assessment activity even when we attempt to frame these lesson observation tutor visits differently, and understandably it often elicits an emotional response from the student teacher. The different approach being used in the research project intended to empower the student teachers to take more ownership of the whole lesson observation process and to create an environment in which the dialogic interactions that take place are more equitably distributed between the parties involved.

The research was exploring how the process of video stimulated reflection (VSR) (Powell, 2005) might be combined with the use of student teachers' bio-pedagogical narratives (Camacho and Fernandez Baloa, 2006), which explore the links between personhood and pedagogy, to provide a new lens through which we could 'see' and analyse practice. Jane had chosen the lesson she wanted to share with me, I did not watch it in advance, either of us could pause the footage at any given moment and with no fixed agenda for what we should be looking for. There were more freedoms than in the standard lesson observation approaches used in most ITE partnerships. By conducting initial bio-pedagogical interviews with the student teachers as part of the research approach, it opened up the possibilities to interrogate the roots and origins of their practice, evident in the captured video footage, relative to what I described as different dimensions of the self. These dimensions might include the educational, cultural, social, political, physical/personal or spiritual and emotional self and how these intersected to shape their evolving pedagogical self, as represented in the video footage. Crucially, one of the purposes of the study was to consider how observing practice in this way might open up a new pedagogical space in ITE for student teachers to really see the responses of young people in their lessons and to particularly consider whether any aspects of their pedagogy were reinforcing potentially inequitable or discriminatory practice. Historically, this has been a recurring problem for the physical education profession, where research has continued to highlight issues in relation to gender (Flintoff, 2011; Flintoff and Scraton, 2006; Hills, 2006; Hills, 2007; Hills and Croston, 2012; Stidder, Lines and Keyworth, 2013), social class (Evans and Davies, 2008); and race and ethnicity (Williams and Bedward, 2001; Kahan, 2003; Dagkas and Benn, 2006; Macdonald and Brooker, 2009).

So, here we were, watching Noor, an adolescent, female, Asian Muslim pupil, employing the most fascinating strategy to avoid getting on the trampoline in a year 9, mixed-sex PE lesson. The video footage allowed us to notice this moment in the first instance as Jane had not seen this while actually teaching the lesson. The pausing of the footage opened up the space for us to begin a discussion around why Noor might not want to get on the trampoline in the first place. It required her to get up in one of the most exposed situations possible in any PE lesson: the sole centre of attention; wearing her PE kit; performing compromising movements in front of boys as well as girls in a way that compromised her modesty. There is also the possibility that Noor may have even been menstruating at that time. This must have been excruciatingly uncomfortable for Noor – no wonder she didn't want to get on the trampoline! Engagement in this activity would have sat counter to her religious beliefs, represented a significant culture clash for her and took no account of her stage of adolescent maturation.

Jane, a caring and sensitive student teacher, was completely mortified at seeing one of her pupils so disengaged. She was initially embarrassed and uncomfortable and I offered her some reassurance that this was a rich opportunity for us to bring to life some of the discussions we had had in taught sessions at university around understanding and valuing difference and diversity the subject area and attending to issues of social justice in PE. We began to explore the difficulties this PE activity created for Noor and then we began to consider why such an activity was being offered to adolescent pupils, in a mixed-sex grouping, to a predominantly Asian, Muslim population of pupils. We discussed the fact that the curriculum had been designed by PE teachers at the school like me and Jane, white British (personal self) and quite comfortable performing physical activities where our bodies are often subject to public scrutiny (cultural and social self). We had done trampolining at school ourselves (educational self) and were quite good at it and in fact we were pretty good at most physical activities we turned our hand to (cultural self), as was probably the case for most of the white British PE teachers at the school in question. Trampolining had also been part of the traditional PE curriculum offer we experienced under the umbrella of gymnastic activities for many years in many schools (educational self). It was often taken for granted that this should be part of the PE experience for young people to offer appropriate balance and breadth. However, the structural conditions in which the pedagogical practice was situated at this school in West London legitimated a curriculum which reinforced inequity and discrimination within the subject culture. The PE curriculum took no account of the religious or cultural backgrounds of the pupils who attended the school and took every account of the backgrounds, interests, experiences and expertise of the PE teachers. The pedagogical actions of teachers have an origin and a history inevitably constrained by dominant political ideologies, requirements of the professional context and the school and subject culture which they are immersed in (Evans, 2004). By choosing to offer trampolining without due consideration for planning and teaching a culturally responsive curriculum, the PE teachers at this school were perpetuating the historical problems in terms of engagement and participation in the subject area.

As a student teacher, Jane did not have the power to change the curriculum offer at her school, so what good was it doing to shine a light on these issues through the use of VSR and exploring, through the associated dialogic interactions, not just Jane's but the shared aspects of our bio-pedagogical narratives? Established literature in the field suggests that the processes of professional socialisation can mitigate against agency and transformation in student teachers (Lortie, 1975; Tabachnick & Zeichner, 1984; Nias, 1989; Maynard, 2001) and PE student teachers more specifically (Lawson, 1983; Curtner-Smith, 1999; Green, 2003). I would argue that our starting point in surfacing discriminatory practice has to be ensuring that we develop the ability, and indeed the pedagogical approaches, to develop the ability to notice it in the first place. Mason (2002), writing in the context of mathematics teaching, raised the significance of developing what he termed as the 'discipline of noticing' and described this concept as being able to be present and sensitive in a given pedagogical moment, having a reason to act in a purposeful way in that moment and subsequently bringing to the fore different and alternative pedagogical practice as a result of exercising discernment in that moment. Discernment involves the ability to judge well and act in relation to those judgements, but judging well is contingent on developing an understanding of what we believe to be the value and purpose of what we are judging in the first place. If we do not understand the contribution of our subject area to the education of young people and how this should be universally inclusive then we are limiting our capacity to judge well in terms of our pedagogical decision making. I would argue that this was evident in the actions of the PE department at this school in West London and then absorbed and replicated by Jane as their student teacher. In teacher education we need to work in new ways with student teachers to raise consciousness in relation to both the unseen as well as the seen influences on our pedagogical practice. Critical dialogue in relation to the political and cultural influences on the curriculum are made more real when connected to observed pedagogical moments in lessons, facilitated by VSR.

Mason goes on to state that discernment is dependent on the teacher's ability to draw on experience and expertise which will support them in making judgements, that should become increasingly sophisticated and subtle as the pedagogical moment is noticed, analysed and then subsequently responded to. This drawing on experience and expertise should involve university tutors or ITE mentors in supporting student teachers to notice key moments in pedagogical practice and then engage them in the kinds of meaningful dialogic interactions which illuminate underlying discourses, which sometimes work against the principles of inclusivity. This will help to disrupt processes which continue to perpetuate the structural inequalities, pedagogical orthodoxies and subject cultures which create barriers to participation and engagement for pupils in their lessons. Until we develop what I would argue is the art rather than the discipline of noticing you cannot raise consciousness and if you are not conscious of inequity you are not positioned to act to address it. We need to recognise as well how our bio-pedagogical narratives, as 'petits recit' or small stories (Hodgson and Standish, 2008, citing Lyotard), offer an invaluable pedagogical resource to support the critical analysis of the influences on our pedagogical practice.

To come full circle, I understand fully why Noor didn't get on the trampoline and more importantly I believe that Jane did too as a result of our VSR session. My hope is that Jane has gone on to become the kind of PE curriculum leader in her future school(s) who seeks to offer a genuinely culturally responsive and inclusive curriculum experience and that we continue to work within the PE profession to ensure that pupils like Noor are never in the position where they have to devise such ingenious strategies to avoid participation in PE. I assume that Noor has never been on a trampoline since she left school but I do hope she has found a way to recognise the value and importance of other types of physical activity as part of a healthy and active lifestyle.

References

Camacho, A. and Fernandez-Balboa, J.M. (2006) 'Ethics, politics and bio-pedagogy in physical education teacher education: easing the tension between the self and the group', *Sport, Education and Society*, 11(1), pp. 1-20.

Curtner-Smith, M. D. (1999) 'The more things change the more they stay the same: factors influencing teachers' interpretations and delivery of National Curriculum Physical Education', *Sport, Education and Society*, 4(1), pp. 75-97.

Dagkas, S. and Benn, T. (2006) 'Young Muslim women's experiences of Islam and physical education in Greece and Britain: a comparative study', *Sport, Education and Society*, 11(1), pp. 21-38.

Evans, J. (2004) 'Making a difference? Education and 'ability' in physical education', *European Physical Education Review*, 10(1), pp. 95-108.

Evans, J. and Davies, B. (2008) 'The poverty of theory: class configurations in the discourse of Physical Education and Health (PEH)', *Physical Education & Sport Pedagogy*, 13(2), pp. 199-213.

Flintoff, A. (2011) 'Gender and learning in PE and Youth Sport', in Armour, K. (ed.) *Introduction to Sports Pedagogy for Teachers and Coaches: Effective learners in Physical Education and Youth Sport*. London: Pearson Publishers.

Flintoff, A. and Fitzgerald, H. (2012) 'Theorising difference and inequality in PE, Youth Sport and Health', in Dowling, F., Fitzgerald, H. and Flintoff, A. (eds.) *Equity and Difference in PE, Sport and Health: A Narrative Approach*. London: Routledge.

Flintoff, A. and Scraton, S. (2006) 'Girls and PE', in Kirk, D., O'Sullivan, M. and Wright, J. (eds.) *An International Handbook on Research in Physical Education*. London: Sage, pp. 767-784.

Green, K. (2003) *Physical Education Teachers on Physical Education: A Sociological Study of Philosophies and Ideologies*. Chester: Chester Academic Press.

Hills, L. (2007) 'Friendship, physicality, and physical education: an exploration of the social and embodied dynamics of girls' physical education experiences', *Sport, Education and Society*, 12(3), pp. 317-336.

Hills, L. (2006) 'Playing the field(s): An exploration of change, conformity and conflict in girls' understandings of gendered physicality in physical education', *Gender and Education*, 18(5), pp. 539-556.

Hills, L. and Croston, A. (2012) "It should be better all together': exploring strategies for 'undoing' gender in coeducational physical education', *Sport Education and Society*, 17(5), pp. 591-605.

Hodgson, N. and Standish, P. (2009) 'Uses and misuses of poststructuralism in educational research', *International Journal of Research & Method in Education*, 32(3), pp. 309-326.

Kahan, D. (2003) 'Islam and physical activity: implications for American sport and physical education', *Journal of Physical Education Recreation and Dance*, 74(3), pp. 48-54.

Lawson, H.A. (1983(b)) 'Toward a model of teacher socialization in physical education: entry into schools, teachers' role orientations, and longevity in teaching (part 2)', *Journal of Teaching in Physical Education*, 3(1), pp. 3-15.

Lortie, D. (1975) *School Teacher: A Sociological Study*. Chicago: University of Chicago Press.

Lyotard, J.F. (1984) *The Postmodern Condition: A Report on Knowledge*. Minneapolis: University of Minnesota Press.

Macdonald, D. and Brooker, R. (1999) 'Articulating a critical pedagogy in physical education teacher education', *Journal of Sport Pedagogy*, 5(1), pp. 51-64.

Mason, J. (2002). *Researching Your Own Practice: The Discipline of Noticing*. (1st ed.). London: Routledge.

Maynard, T. (2001) 'The student teacher and the school community of practice: a consideration of 'learning as participation'', *Cambridge Journal of Education*, 31, pp. 39-52.

Nias, J. (1989) 'Teaching and the self', in Holly, M. and McLaughlin, C. (eds.) *Perspectives on Teachers' Professional Development*.

Lewes: Falmer.

Powell, E. (2005) 'Conceptualising and facilitating active learning: teachers' video-stimulated reflective dialogues', *Reflective Practice*, 6(3), pp. 407-418.

Stidder, G., Lines, G. and Keyworth, S. (2013) 'Investigating the gender regime in physical education and dance', in Stidder, G. and Hayes, S. (eds.) *Equity and Inclusion in Physical Education and Sport*. 2nd edition edn. Oxon: Routledge, pp. 66-86.

Tabachnick, B. and Zeichner, K. (1984) 'The impact of the student teaching experience on the development of teacher perspectives', *Journal of Teacher Education*, 35, pp. 28-36.

Williams, A. and Bedward, J. (2001) 'Gender, culture and the generation gap: student and teacher perceptions of aspects of national curriculum physical education', *Sport, Education and Society*, 6(1), pp. 53-66.

The voice of educators and education students

Benjamin Zephaniah

Benjamin Zephaniah has written poetry books for children and adults, and novels for teenagers. As well as writing plays for stage, radio, and television, he is constantly touring with his music band The Revolutionary Minds. He is also an actor, radio, and television presenter, and his passions are animal rights, human rights, and Kung Fu. He is Professor of Poetry and Creative Writing at Brunel University.

The voice of educators and education students

Civil Lies

Benjamin Zephaniah

Dear Teacher,
When I was born in Ethiopia,
Life began,
As I sailed down the Nile, civilization began.
When I stopped to think, universities were built,
When I set sail,
Asian and true Americans sailed with me.

When we traded, nations were built,
We did not have animals,
Animals lived with us,
We had so much time,
Thirteen months made our year,
We created social services,
And cities that still stand.

So teacher do not say,
Columbus discovered me,
Check the great things I was doing,
Before I suffered slavery.
Yours truly,

Mr Africa

Benjamin Zephaniah
First published in Talking Turkeys by Viking Books 1994

For Word

Thank you for the words I read
Thank you for the words I need
Thank you for the WORDS so great
Thanks for words that raise debate,
Thanks for the words on my bookshelf
Thanx for the words I make myself
Thank you for words that make me cry
And words that leave me feeling dry.

Thanks for WORDS that do inspire
And those words that burn like fire
Thanks for all the words I note
Thank you for all the words I quote,
I thank you for the words like me
Thanks for WORDS that set me free
And I thank you for words like you
I always need a word or two.

Thanks for words that make things plain
And words that help me to explain
Thanks for words that make life fun

The voice of educators and education students

And words that help me overcome,
Thanks for words that make me rap
Thanks for words that make me clap
Thanks for words that make me smile
Thanks for words with grace and style.

Thanks for all those words that sing
Thanks for words are everything
Thanks for all the words like this
And little sloppy words like kiss,
Thanks for words like hip-hooray
And those cool words I like to say
Thanks for words that reach and touch
Thank you very, very much.

Benjamin Zephaniah
First published in Funky Chickens by Viking Books 1996

The voice of educators and education students

Phil Renshaw   Jenny Robinson

Cranfield School of Management

Henley Business School

Dr Phil Renshaw and Jenny Robinson are academics, entrepreneurs and teachers. Phil and Jenny met on the first day of their PhDs and immediately realised that they shared a depth of business experience from around the world that, combined with coaching, provided a unique perspective on leaders and their leadership. They both teach Research Philosophy at Cranfield School of Management and other UK Universities. The way that Research Philosophy is taught and made interesting has become an abiding passion for them both, giving rise to new articles and ideas to help students of the future grapple with the subject more successfully than Jenny and Phil did in their own early-academic years. Jenny is finishing her PhD at Henley Business School. Together, Phil and Jenny co-authored Coaching on the Go (Pearson, 2019).

The voice of educators and education students

ON BEING DONALD TRUMP: How gamification helps research philosophy make sense. [OR] the surprising link to your research philosophy

Phil Renshaw & Jenny Robinson

Photo by Library of Congress

If you are a potential or existing Masters or PhD student, you may not know what it is yet, but your research philosophy is a fundamental building block of your studies. Your educational success relies upon it. If you teach Research Methods, we think this will be useful to you too. And, surprisingly, Donald Trump can help you all! Read on…

The voice of educators and education students

Just for now, before reading further, stand up and BE Donald Trump. If you can, put aside your evaluative mind (stop questioning why we're asking), and instead engage your experiential mind and just BE Donald Trump. Stand like he stands; look at the world through his eyes; see what he sees. Really settle into this other-person experience and engage the world with all your senses as if you are him. Imagine his famous mop of blonde (or yellow?) hair. Feel your (allegedly) little hands. And ask yourself: how do I feel? What does the world look like? What is truth and what is fake (news)? You may not like the idea of doing this, most likely if you're not a Trump supporter, but try it out. It works. It will help you make sense of and gain more from this chapter. Go on, please do it now for a minute. Stand-up.

Please, continue to embody Donald Trump as you return to seated and now write down your thoughts, as Donald, by completing these sentences:

- People, in general, are …
- The world is …
- My opinion is …
- Your opinion is …
- I know I'm right when …
- I know you are right when …

OK. Thank you. You can relax and be yourself again. Now consider all the ways in which the answers you gave above as Donald Trump are the same or different to answers you would have given as yourself?

We have asked hundreds of doctoral students to do this exercise and we've had some fascinating responses as to how they see the world as Donald. These include,

- ✔ I'm right and you're wrong
- ✔ I'm invincible
- ✔ Women are not important
- ✔ I am all powerful
- ✔ I've got no idea what's really going on
- ✔ Why are you other people even here?
- ✔ What I say goes
- ✔ Whatever you think. I am the truth
- ✔ If the evidence does not support my view, then the evidence is wrong.

As hinted in the title of this essay, we are keen to find ways – some of them unconventional – to engage students and researchers in Research Philosophy. It is not a field of study with a reputation for fun, but we are working hard to change all that. In this chapter, we explore how gamification can be used to help put the fun, and greater understanding, into a critical element of Masters and Doctoral research training, namely: *what is your research philosophy and what difference does it make*?

Understanding the answers to these questions has been described as a key learning leap in the doctoral journey (Wisker et al., 2010). In other words, without successfully grappling with this you will not achieve the desired educational progress. So, what is a research philosophy? Drawing on inspiration from, inter alia, Kuhn (1970), Lather (2006) and Saunders et al (2019) we consider a research philosophy to be a constellation of beliefs and assumptions that together lead to a series of research choices which enable the understanding, explanation and development of knowledge. By this we mean your set of beliefs and assumptions. How you, as a researcher, see and understand the world. This will incorporate many ideas and constructs that you are very unlikely to have thought about before: *what is reality? How do you know? What is acceptable as proof that something is true?* And it will introduce lots of horribly long and undoubtedly confusing words and concepts that you will need to get to grips with: *what is your ontology? your epistemology? Are you a postmodernist or maybe a positivist?*

Masters level students are normally expected to engage in identifying their research philosophy because it informs their research method, a crucial part of most Masters level programmes and something which feeds into their final dissertation. We know that not all courses push this hard, but it is a core section in most Research Methods modules – or it should be. If you have not already been directed to do so, you might want to check out our friend Mark Saunders' best-selling book, and specifically chapter 4 (Saunders, Lewis and Thornhill, 2019). In fact, you can download this chapter for free. This is a book worth your investment of time and attention.

Doctoral students, meanwhile, are expected to defend their thesis and talk with knowledge and conviction about their approach to their research: this includes explaining their research philosophy and the choices that it engenders. They must be able to defend their view of the world and any implications for their research choices – the method. As recent PhD students, during our training we noticed that we, and our peers, struggled with ways to even broach this subject – it was complex, obtuse, and time consuming and besides knowing that it might come up as a point of issue in our Viva, we could not immediately see the point. We sat in lectures in which very clever people used very long words in sentences that made sense in the moment, but often not so afterwards. Thus, we needed to find our own way through this. And so our foray into teaching research philosophy began.

Generally, students are drilled with standard questions that are used with such frequency that they assume the status of mantras: *What is your research question? Does your methodology allow you to answer your research question?* Although important, these questions miss the deeper point of research philosophy: *How do you see the world? How does how you see the world shape how you approach your research? How is your research question shaped by your world view? What literature do you select to read or not read as a consequence of this view? What conversations will you take part in and ultimately what is the contribution to knowledge you will make?* After all. What is 'knowledge' anyway?

In short, how does evidence turn into knowledge and what constitutes truth?

Which leads back to the Donald Trump experience. This is the first game we play in our Research Philosophy workshops that aims to help researchers recognise that there are different ways to see the world and that through different viewpoints what counts as truth and evidence might change. Some researchers speak of President Trump as having built a successful business empire and therefore his instincts for making policy to encourage free enterprise can be relied upon. Other researchers consider past success and instinct unreliable ways to decide on how to proceed. These orthogonal views stimulate discussion and debate around the fundamental questions that underpin research, can we believe it? And does it add to our knowledge? Clearly, some people think that certain types of evidence matter, and other types of evidence don't. Most importantly, are we even aware of these differences!

Our central argument is: that research philosophy matters. It should sit at the core of research design not at the periphery. You need to start your research journey with this question and these issues, not simply add them in at the end as may often happen –

The voice of educators and education students

which people tell us (not unsurprisingly once you know) can create conflicts and nightmares. Learning about research philosophy gives insight into hidden perspectives and how they impact the whole process of research. We have sought to add a voice to this important idea and to move academia closer to a union of teaching and learning research philosophy by adding games that engage and challenge.

Of course, if you are a Trump supporter you may feel that our method is unfair, biased or plain wrong. We acknowledge that there are risks here. We know that we, like everyone else, bring our own biases to play both here in this exercise and in our own research. Ironically, that's the whole point of this chapter. However, when we do this exercise and when we asked you to do it, we do not feel we lead anyone to describing and identifying their feelings and we do not lead them as to what they share with us. The bottom line is that most people are very aware of Donald Trump and often hold clear opinions about his opinions/perspectives and this is what we're trying to draw out. Life and its consequences, including research, often looks very different through the eyes of Donald Trump. To offer a simple example, if you are researching climate change the very questions you will ask will be different to the mainstream if you hold the same views as Donald Trump. You may, for example, research why so many people believe something that is plainly wrong (in his eyes).

Another "game" that we play is to use small group discussions centred on the textbook by Blaikie (2007) - this is a standard University text and is one of several that can be used for this exercise (Renshaw et al., 2018). In these groups, an individual randomly draws a 'philosophy card' and this is used to provoke them to talk through the specific lens on the card and its potential impact on their own research. As a consequence, it is not unusual to find committed positivists stretching themselves to re-construct their research through the lens of critical studies; or interpretivists considering how hermeneutics might throw new light on their research (look, long strange words are appearing – sorry). It is unlikely that at the point they are struggling with these reversals of ontology and epistemology (more strange words) that they would say it is FUN, but games that discombobulate also stimulate. (And being Donald Trump always gets a laugh). Afterall, the key to learning is to do something beyond just passively taking in information. So if you don't know what an interpretivist or a positivist is, look it up, find one to talk to, and think about whether it applies to you.

Theory and experience demonstrate that gamification adds fun and relevance. We collect comments after our workshops and have been gratified to read:

- *I have just had an epiphany'*
- *'I have realised that there is a boundary to my research question that I had not previously identified'*
- *A 'different paradigm can completely change [a] paper because it changes [the] focus of research'*
- *'I am now redesigning my research…using different methodologies that will provide richer data.'*
- *'I discovered that it might be valuable to consider and explore the influence of my presence, the questions I asked, and the concepts I introduced on participants' answers during the semi-structured interviews I conducted'*

We sincerely hope that a renewed focus on teaching this discipline will help other doctoral students survive and enjoy the research philosophy journey too. If you want to understand more, or play our learning games, please get in touch. And, in case you're interested, one of us is now a critical realist and the other a pragmatist – 4 years ago we had never even heard of these terms!!

References

Blaikie, N. (2007) *Approaches to Social Enquiry: Advancing Knowledge*. Cambridge: Polity Press.

Kuhn, T.S. (1970) *The Structure of Scientific Revolutions*. University of Chicago Press.

Lather, P. (2006) 'Paradigm proliferation as a good thing to think with: teaching research in education as a wild profusion', *International Journal of Qualitative Studies in Education*, 19(1), pp.35–57.

Renshaw, P. St. J., Robinson, J., Parry, E. and Saunders, M. N. K. (2018) 'Standing in the shoes of giants: teaching research philosophy', *BAM Conference,* University of West England, UK.

Saunders, M. N. K., Lewis, P. and Thornhill, A. (2019) *Research Methods for Business Students*. 8th edn. Pearson Education Limited.

Wisker, G., Morris, C., Cheng, M., Masika, R., Warnes, M., Trafford, V., Robinson, G. and Lilly, J. (2010) *Doctoral Learning Journeys Final Report*. York: HEA.

Mike Watts

Mike Watts is Professor of Education at Brunel, conducting 'naturalistic' people-orientated research principally in science education, learning technologies and scholarship in higher education. He has conducted major studies in both formal and informal educational settings in the UK and abroad and has published widely through numerous books, journal articles and conference papers. He teaches at all levels within Brunel's Department of Education and currently supervises 13 PhD students. He was raised and educated in Wales, is a native Welsh speaker and a passionate supporter of Welsh rugby. He loves, too, spending time in Italy and is (slowly) learning Italian.

The voice of educators and education students ─────────

Should we be educating for activism?

Mike Watts

Holly Gillibrand leaves school for an hour every Friday to demand action on climate change. She lives in Fort William in Scotland (population 10,000) and is joined in her protests by 40 people every Friday, trying to persuade the Scottish government to "actually do something". Ella and Caitlin McEwan are sisters from Southampton who raised a petition asking fast food restaurants to stop putting plastic toys in children's meals. They gathered more than 400,000 signatures and since then, McDonalds offers customers a choice between a toy or a fruit. Burger King said it will remove the plastic toys altogether. The September 2019 climate strikes, formally the Global Week for the Future, were a series of international strikes and protests by school children to demand that action should be taken to address climate change. The organising groups reported that roughly 7.6 million people, young and old, participated in the events.

What does this have to do with education? Well, arguably, our role as educators is to teach young people about morals and values, about what is right and what is wrong, where to draw the line, how to make decisions, take action and solve 'real life' problems. The questions debated in the media are: When young people take time off their studies to join a protest, are they jeopardising or enhancing their education? Will they learn more or less by being absent from lessons and joining with millions of others in strike action? The following quote is taken from a famous book on education, *Teaching as a Subversive Activity*, published back in 1969 and written by American educationalists Neil Postman and Charles Weingartner:

> *School is the one institution in our society that is inflicted on everybody, and what happens in school makes a difference – for good or ill. We use the word "inflicted" because we believe that the way schools are currently conducted does very little, and quite probably nothing, to help us solve any or even some of the [world's] problems (p.xiii).*

My own views on this are clear: schools are no better now than they were in 1969 in tackling major problems such as climate change. I am certain, too, that young people gain far more from the positive experiences of participating in peaceful, powerful protest than sitting in school classrooms. Teenagers must be able to form, express and share their views - and adults must learn to listen. Protest has a valuable place in a civilised, democratic society - historically much good has come from it. But the questions that follow from this are: Should we educators pick up on the implications behind Postman and Weingartner's quote, and actually *teach* young people to be activists? Should this teaching be done in schools and universities?

To get going I want to explore the notion of transgression – what it means to transgress or to be transgressive. This has been a thread of discussion within our Department of Education for some while, particularly through the writings of Nic Crowe and Gail

Waite. When we want students to be (nicely) transgressive (i.e. be creative) we ask them to shift the boundaries, push the envelope, be off the wall, think outside the box, go where others haven't been, be outlandish, be radical thinkers and so on. This level of transgression is what Nic has called 'transgressive lite'. Most undergraduate or M-level research studies have this in common, they are usually explorations of some educational issue that has already been researched in one form or another – but maybe not quite like this. At doctoral level, this is a clear and essential requirement: a PhD is awarded (in large part) for its 'unique contribution to knowledge in the field'. In this respect, students are expected to be 'transgressive' by going beyond educational designs, theories, outcomes, recommended practices and so on, and in then adding something new of their own to the mix. There is also, of course, the other side to transgression. When (maybe the same?) students are *undesirably* transgressive (anti-social), we say that they have *really* overstepped the mark, are out of line, off limits, out of order, crossed the Rubicon, know no boundaries, off the scale or are 'beyond the pale'. We might approve of (grin, smile at) bizarre activities as 'transgression lite' and yet thoroughly disapprove of other activities that are 'very wide of the mark'. So, there are even boundaries within transgression – it is possibly acceptable to tip-toe over the line and dazzle people with 'cutting edge' theatre, 'fusion' or offbeat music, wacky art or quirky (creative) writing – but it is not acceptable to be completely weirdo, to fracture social etiquette, flout rules and regulations, to deeply offend or bully other people, be violent or extremist. One argument here is that it is an important part of teaching and learning to appreciate what and where particular 'lines' are drawn, and in deciding what to do about them: when breaking the rules is acceptable or not. And whether you care about being accepted or not.

Back to environmental issues and climate change. The United Nations World Summit in 2005 set out three 'pillars of sustainability': the economic, social and environmental factors that should be taken into consideration. Sustainability involves the careful management of resources and care of the environment and – as we exercise that care - the three factors are clearly interconnected, overlapping and interdependent within a cultural context. Education for sustainable development, then, is the process of equipping people with the knowledge and understanding, skills and attributes needed to work and live in a way that safeguards environmental, social and economic wellbeing, both in the present and for future generations. At Brunel, issues of sustainability are being introduced as a component of all degree courses. This will entail identifying areas for the integration of sustainability teaching in undergraduate and postgraduate programmes and modules. Sustainable ideas taught during sessions are essential precursors to those that can be implemented in the practice of future professionals. I am all for this and for example, I believe people should consider what environmental stewardship means in the context of our/their own professional and personal lives. They should develop a future-facing outlook, learn to think about the consequences of actions, and how systems and societies can be adapted to ensure sustainable futures. At a small, local level, Hutchins and White's (2009) 'five Rs' waste hierarchy model describes the various ways in which people can act more sustainably: reducing, recycling, reusing, rethinking and researching. It might be somewhat local and personal, but it can be very far-reaching.

In my view, however, educating for sustainability goes beyond the mere knowledge of science, social and economic content and context. It should be understood as the ability to engage critically with, make informed decisions about - and take action on -

environment-related issues. Critical thinking and active engagement should be emphasised as important learning outcomes along with fundamental literacy, knowledge and competences and a broad understanding of sustainability. I think people - young and old - really need to form their own understandings – to know enough and feel sufficiently confident about changes to our environment to go protesting. They should question, in a very critical and sceptical way, the information about climate change being fed through social and conventional media, by teachers at school - or university level for that matter. That is, people should take responsibility and control over their own learning about current environmental topics, use as many sources and multi-media resources as possible to build awareness in order to achieve action. As educators, we not only have a role in enabling people to know about the extent of climate crises and arming them with information and opinions, we should also teach how to respond, with tactics that range from volunteering and raising money to boycotting and marching. They need to know about the conventional approaches such as voting, lobbying, petitions and protests. But, when those approaches fail (as they oft times do) then there must also be recourse to non-violent, disruptive civil disobedience.

So, does teaching for sustainability also involve teaching for activism? Just how transgressive (lite or otherwise) should that teaching be? What if activism becomes anti-social, begins to interfere with transport or impinge on people's ability to get to work, causing havoc and inconvenience? All answers on a postcard, please. I leave the arguments here with a second quote from Postman and Weingartner:

> *Clearly, there is no more important function for education to fulfil than that of helping us recognise the world we actually live*

in and simultaneously, of helping us to master concepts that will increase our ability to cope with it. This is the essential criterion for judging the relevance of all education (p.212).

What was true in 1969 is just as transgressively true fifty years later.

References

Hutchins, D. and White, S. (2009) 'Coming round to recycling', *British Medical Journal,* 338, pp. 746– 748.

Postman, N. and Wiengartner, C. (1969) *Teaching as a Subversive Activity.* New York, Delta Publishing Co.

The voice of educators and education students

Yujuan Luo

There are a lot of 'tags' on me, including a student, a teacher, a daughter, a friend, a colleague or a mentor, to name a few. Here for this special book, I consider myself as an online tutor who can share some personal reflections to anyone who has the opportunity to read this book. Especially, at the time of writing this bio, the Coronavirus outbreak is regarded as a pandemic. It is a heart-breaking moment, but for educators, it is also a time to reflect on mobile pedagogy to the best benefits for high-quality online education. By now, mobile learning is not a matter of choice, but a necessity. As an editor of this particular book, I take the privilege to share my thoughts of the great advantages of being in a digital age.

The voice of educators and education students

What should we expect of online learning and teaching under the background of the Coronavirus outbreak?

Yujuan Luo

The coronavirus outbreak in China is disheartening and has brought profound changes to Chinese society, not only concerning the development of the national or global economy but also regarding education. Every year, February is the beginning of a new term for students nationwide. There is, therefore, a large scale of student migration. This year, however, February has been a very quiet and dark moment for people in China because of the worsening situation of the coronavirus outbreak. China is on lockdown and the whole world is watching the development of the outbreak in real-time. Given the contagious nature of this new deadly virus, students and workers must stay at home. The commencement of school terms, therefore, has been delayed indefinitely, leading to an increase in the demand for online learning and working.

It has been some time since the emergence of online education, which has been significantly promoted in higher education. It is not

The voice of educators and education students

until the recent coronavirus outbreak that this learning approach has been widely adopted and become the mainstream teaching method. In the most affected regions, based on the country's previous experience with SARS, there is a significant chance that schools and universities face the prospect of losing the whole semester or more. Given this situation, the Ministry of Education (MOE, 2020) has called a halt to in-person teaching and is promoting online education to minimise human-to-human interaction. As a result, schools at all levels, including universities, have been promoting e-learning or e-teaching strategies. The Ministry also has been working to launch a national internet cloud classroom this month, which would include teaching resources and courses available for students and teachers. The image below is news from the People's Daily, China.

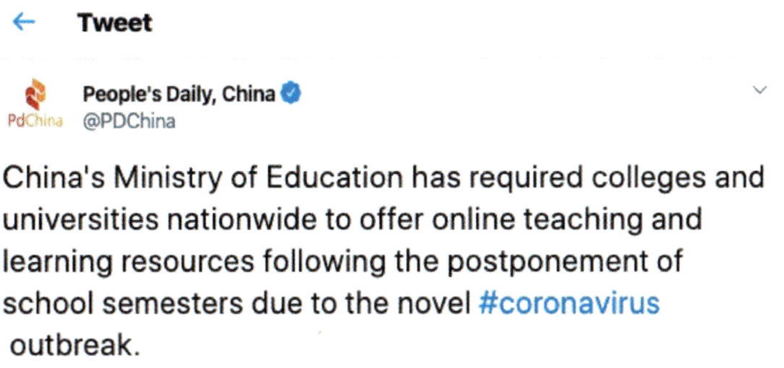

← **Tweet**

People's Daily, China ✓
@PDChina

China's Ministry of Education has required colleges and universities nationwide to offer online teaching and learning resources following the postponement of school semesters due to the novel #coronavirus outbreak.

Figure 1: A screenshot of a tweet from the People's Daily China regarding the online teaching and learning suggested by MOE.

The mixed pictures of e-higher education – students learning full time from home

Although students may find this innovative learning convenient, they still question the effectiveness of online learning. Students comment that they have more freedom when studying at home, but they can also be easily distracted and lose motivation. Teachers, generally speaking, will have to learn something new and consider it a novelty. Online teaching, according to many teachers in China, is regarded as a supplement, not a necessity. Due to the national health emergency, teachers must learn to speak naturally in front of a camera and motivate and engage students in a virtual space. This is not easy for some teachers who are used to the traditional approach to teaching. According to Dr Liu, a university teacher living in Xi'an, an area that has been seriously affected, 'There is no choice that we have but to go online. But this is quite challenging, although we have been given some training on how to conduct live-streaming courses beforehand'. Some more issues emerged on the first day of national online teaching, 17th February, which is considered 'the back to school' day of many universities. Even though teachers and students are keen and prepared to embrace this new approach, the E-Systems that offer online courses, including MOOC and Rain Classroom, broke down on the first day because the massive number of users caused overloading issues. The current status quo has made online learning the main mode of learning instead of a supplementary approach to learning. This poses several challenges to the implementation of online learning.

Advantages and challenges for the implementation of online streaming courses in Chinese society

There are several benefits of this new approach to teaching and learning, including convenience, flexibility, personalisation, engagement, hands-on life skills, life-long learning and seamlessness. Students feel more comfortable participating in the online-streaming classroom, and therefore more engaged with their online teachers in collaborative and individualised learning environments. They may choose a comfortable place to embark on their learning. They can listen to the online-streaming courses multiple times, so that they fully understand their courses and

The voice of educators and education students

can interact with teachers whenever they have questions without interrupting instructors. The image below is a screenshot of a synchronous teacher-student interaction.

There are probably more advantages of mobile technology-based courses based on students' individual needs and motivations. Students can develop their personalised learning approach. For instance, they can follow up with any topics that teachers introduce based on their personal interest and contexts. They can also learn at their own pace in order to fully understand the lessons. Moreover, students may feel less anxious to post questions during the online courses compared to traditional face-to-face lectures. In this way, the learning could be more effective and interactive. However, the online-streaming course may not work for all students. Students who lack self-discipline may be easily distracted by their daily chores. According to Dr Liu, who has experienced this new type of live-streaming course, the table below demonstrates how much time his students spend engaged with the online course. Notably, several students were only engaged with teachers for less than 10 minutes. This raises issues regarding the quality of online-streaming courses. A lack of supervision could explain students' disengagement.

Figure 2: An example of a teacher-student interaction during an online streaming lesson.

The voice of educators and education students

Students' number QQ号码	The time being attentive in the online course (minutes) 听课总时长(分钟)	进出房间详细记录[上课终
3319613018	97	(10:24:17-12:00:57[iOS])
1433198231	98	(10:22:44-10:26:32[Web])(
1062702315	98	(10:20:15-10:38:36[Androi
1260528560	95	(10:24:17-10:35:51[Androi
739201426	92	(10:29:03-11:50:54[PC])(11
1453870901	103	(10:17:34-10:20:45[PC])(1(
1376102039	97	(10:23:28-10:25:31[PC])(1(
1174453512	100	(10:19:14-10:30:19[iOS])(1
1677210240	101	(10:20:07-12:00:57[PC])
626682471	104	(10:17:01-12:00:57[H5])
2686624973	102	(10:18:34-12:00:57[PC])
212726899	106	(10:14:54-12:00:57[PC])
1341325719	84	(10:30:19-10:54:41[H5])(1C
872417537	83	(10:31:34-10:49:24[Androi
1850095409	84	(10:35:51-10:45:23[H5])(1C
1577218636	102	(10:19:14-12:00:57[Web])
2131116815	93	(10:24:28-11:33:36[H5])(11
526509262	12	(10:17:34-10:29:49[H5])
2044767029	102	(10:18:34-12:00:57[PC])
1789233130	103	(10:17:01-10:19:37[H5])(1C
3142612989	103	(10:17:34-10:26:02[Web])(
2938188724	92	(10:25:48-10:28:18[H5])(1C
1542089034	1	(10:17:34-10:18:40[H5])(1C
2453476570	100	(10:20:45-11:15:31[Web])(
614220700	87	(10:18:40-10:25:48[Web])(
943956418	104	(10:17:01-12:00:57[Web])
1151489825	102	(10:18:40-12:00:57[PC])
1035415072	104	(10:17:01-12:00:57[PC])
2731157026	13	(10:17:27-10:30:03[H5])
1362583204	97	(10:22:55-10:23:28[PC])(1C

Figure 3: A screenshot of students' active participation in the online streaming lesson.

Additionally, online-streaming teaching must deal with technical failure due to insufficient technological infrastructure. According to another teacher, Dr Yin, 'We had to cancel the lessons on the first day we initiated the online teaching strategy because many students failed to get connected. Ideally, online streaming lessons should be video-based like face-to-face communication, which I

37

can still see students' reactions. But due to the technical failure, as a compromising solution, the course has been changed to audio-based. In this way, we no longer can see students' reaction and do not know what they are doing with this online streaming lesson'.

In sum, China is confronted with several challenges similar to challenges faced in other parts of the world, including poor infrastructure, financial constraints, inadequate support and resistance from teachers (Khan et al., 2012; Kisanga & Ireson, 2015). China also faces some unique challenges, including barriers from traditional culture, an uneven level of information literacy and a lack of favourable e-learning environments (Wang, Liu & Zhang, 2018). Specifically, from the perspective of traditional culture, teachers are viewed as authorities who impart knowledge and students are inclined to accept knowledge passively. Online learning differs from traditional teaching in many aspects, including the learning environment and learning objects and approaches. The two distinctive learning approaches pose challenges for both teachers and students who have grown accustomed to the traditional learning approach. It seems that both teachers and students are not fully prepared to go completely online. Some teachers who are not ready for online teaching are struggling to solve technical problems, including using novel gadgets and software even though they have had only a few training sessions online. They do not have enough time to digest and put their training into practice, which affects the effectiveness of this new approach. The notion of unfavourable e-learning environments refers to technological infrastructure and the regional disparity of e-learning development. Schools in big cities generally have more ICT facilities than those in remote or rural areas where it is very difficult to implement online learning strategies. Teachers' resistance and lack of ICT knowledge are considered another challenge to establishing favourable e-learning environments.

Implications

After more than a decade of development that has led China to make significant progress and achievements in the infrastructure, market growth and number of users engaged in e-learning and online learning, the coronavirus outbreak can be considered a litmus test for the progression and results of e-learning and online learning development. Much needs to be done in the future to tackle the issues and challenges of online learning, including providing high-quality teacher training, sharing effective e-learning resources and consolidating technological infrastructures. Until stakeholders are physically able and mentally ready to accept and adopt this new approach, the results will be far from satisfactory. Just as Zhangyuan Du, Vice Minister of Education, suggests, there are three key tasks for Chinese e-learning advancement, which are: teachers' and students' acknowledgement of online learning, teachers' competence integrating ICT with daily teaching and the production of high-quality resources that help teachers focus on pedagogical design (Liu, 2015).

References

Liu, Y. D. (2015) *Speech at the international conference on educational informatics* [in Chinese]. China Education Newspaper 06 September: 1

Khan, S. H., Hasan, M. and Clement, C. K. (2012) 'Barriers to the introduction of ICT into education in developing countries: the example of Bangladesh', *International Journal of Instruction*. 5(2), pp. 61-80.

Kisanga, D. & Ireson, G. (2015) 'Barriers and strategies on adoption of E-learning in Tanzanian higher learning institutions: lessons for adopters', *International Journal of Education and Development Using Information and Communication Technology*, 11(2), pp. 126-137.

Ministry of Education (2020) *MOE issues instructions for deployment of HEI online teaching* [online]. Available from: http://en.moe.gov.cn/news/press_releases/202002/t20200208_419136.html (Accessed 20 February 2020).

Wang, Y., Liu, X. and Zhang, Z. (2018) 'An overview of E-learning in China: history, challenges and opportunities', *Research in Comparative and International Education,* 13(1), pp.195-210. Available from: doi: 10.1177/1745499918763421.

Nic Crowe

When Nic isn't up to mischief with his friend Cayla, he writes stories about the digital lives of children and young people. And sometimes he finds time for teaching as well.

The voice of educators and education students

That perfect girl is gone…

Nic Crowe

These are exciting times for those of us who like our Education with a distinctive Princess flavour. Christmas 2019 saw the release of the second instalment of the Disney box office behemoth *Frozen,* whilst in early 2020 the eagerly anticipated live-action version of *Mulan* will hit UK multiplexes. Along with the 2017 reboot of *Beauty and the Beast* (much closer to the darker Leprince de Beaumont story than the 1992 Animation) this quadrangle of narratives represent the most feminist of the Disney fantasy. Of course, all the required themes are there: the transience of beauty, the folly of vanity, the importance of commitment to friends and family and of course the romantic idealism that love can conquer all. In *Frozen*, however the later is subverted in so far as it appears to marginalise the emphasis on heterosexual courtship in favour of the powerful love between the two sisters. When Elsa shimmies her way through the emerging ice palace singing that 'the perfect girl is gone' it is not just a rejection of her traditional notions of girlhood but also the representations of the previous Disney princesses within which it has been enshrined. In this sense, Elsa offers a proactive, ambitious heroine of sorts with both a voice and a desire for adventure embodying the *Barbie* hashtag 'a girl can be anything she wants to be' – even 'wicked'.

In his book 'The Uses of Enchantment' psychologist Bruno Bettelheim observes that the human spirit requires the dark fantasy of fairy stories through which to discover and make sense of our humanity. In this sense, the seemingly unattainable and impossible juxtaposition of Belle and the Beast, or Elsa and Anna, provide an arena in which we can unpick and reflect on our own relationships and attitudes. As Bettelheim reminds us fairy tales are not just for children. They are important cultural devices that offer us opportunities to develop a greater sense of meaning and purpose about our own lives. Putting the Disney re-telling aside, the animated fantasies of Studio Ghibli (which began streaming on Netflix at the start of the year) arguably offer some of the best examples of the contemporary fairytale. Lauded by film critics and cultural commentators alike, yet comparatively ignored by the majority of the general public in the UK, Japan's Studio Ghibli has much to offer the Educationalist, as a number of our undergraduate dissertations have begun to explore.

Founded in 1985 by visionary director Hayao Miyazaki, Ghibli boasts endless standing ovations at festivals, the two highest ever grossing home-produced films in Japan (*'Spirited Away'* 2002, *'Princess Mononoke'*, 1997) and perhaps most importantly to Miyazaki himself, an Oscar for Best Animated Feature (*'Spirited Away'*) at the 75th Academy Awards. Not bad for a studio that claimed to make each film without a script, allowing the story to take shape through its storyboards. Often compared to Disney (who ironically now virtually control the company through Western distribution rights), Ghibli offers a distinctly Japanese flavour to their animation which is kept pure by a strict 'no cuts' policy for its western distribution (Miyazaki's *'Nausicaa of the Valley of the Wind'* was savaged for its US release). Whilst Disney can perhaps claim the monopoly on the animated retreading of the classic tales of rags to riches – as attested by the plethora of Disney Princess merchandise in their stores – Ghibli craft an altogether different kind of narrative. Like the fairy tales of old, Miyazaki's plots often revolve around cautionary themes - environmental issues, anti-war, the illusion of physical beauty - albeit in a more multi-layered, somewhat holistic, package.

Take *Howls Moving Castle* for example. Loosely based on the novel from the (arguably forgotten) Welsh treasure Diane Wynne Jones, the film tells the tale of young Sophie Hatter who is transformed into an old woman by a witch and who in the process of looking for a cure, is forced to housekeep for the flighty and vane wizard Howl. An almost 'Beauty and the Beast' in reverse in which the hero eventually learns to love the cursed heroine, *Howls Moving Castle* centres on a text familiar to many folk tales, that of coming of age. Often this is explained in terms of the dangers of sexual awakening – for Belle the beast is a metaphor for a predatory lover, similarly we watch a childish Elsa transform into a woman's body as she learns to 'let it go' and accept her powers – but here Miyazaki and Wynne Jones approach it from a different angle. Eighteen-year-old Sophie is forced to put aside the trappings of childhood and youth. As she adjusts to her aged body, she unbiddingly learns the qualities that accompany old age and experience; the ability to see through nonsense, feistiness, fearlessness, peace and an appreciation that beauty takes many forms. As the tale progresses, we see that, depending on her situation and mood, Sophie can exercise some control over the curse of agedness as she shifts back and forth between various representations of womanhood; the teenage girl, a shriveled crone, a dignified old lady and a girl with premature greying hair. In the middle of the film, in the guise of the latter, Sophie reveals to Howl that she feels ugly. When he replies that he finds her beautiful she immediately reverts to the crone representation as a defence against his advances.

Miyazaki crafts a cautionary message then that suggests we learn to appreciate the virtues of growing old and that beauty comes in stages. The tension between age and beauty is a recurrent analytical theme across a range of writing. Bodies are of course emblemic – important sites of both identity and of cultural meaning. In his book, 'The body social: Symbolism, self and society' Anthony Synnott observes that *"The body is not a 'given' but a social category with different meanings imposed and developed by every age and by different sectors of the population. As such it is therefore sponge-like in its ability to absorb meanings" (1993:1)*. Yet as Judith Butler also reminds us, this is nearly always understood as a comparison between the 'real' and the 'ideal'. Thus, whilst some bodies are considered legitimate, others are not and since they are socially constructed they facilitate or deny particular forms of identity.

According to Karen Dias, body image remains a central issue in third wave feminism if only because all women, feminist or not, have a range of heartfelt and complex emotions on the topic. Rather than assuming the legal and political struggles that had defined much of the preceding feminist agenda, third wave feminism directed its focus onto popular cultural texts and their impact on the subjective experiences of women because these represent the most visible obstacles to female emancipation. Popular culture has focused a great deal of attention on women and their bodies, particularly in terms of what constitutes youth, health and beauty. The female body is expressed as a site of contradiction and ambivalence, revered simultaneously as a 'Diet Goddess' – the icon of health, restraint and perseverance - and demonised as a 'Food Failure' – the embodiment of excess and lack of control. Women's bodies are thus objectified and subjected to control, admiration, criticism and re-articulation across the media. There are contradictions in terms of how this is then articulated on page and screen. So on the one hand health professionals bombard us with warnings around size and weight in which beauty is expressed in what seems to be solely numerical terms; yet on another Gok Wan is granted almost god-like status for teaching women to be comfortable in their body whatever its shape; whilst the young women in the pro-ana community are clinicised and sanitized for offering an alternate, trangressive expression of beauty.

Like modern Disney, Ghibli cannot sit outside such tensions. Japanese animation is recognized for its use of pre-pubescent and adolescent girl and androgynous male characters often referred to as Shojo. In the West, wide-eyes, wasp like waists and high foreheads are seen to define the genre creating a representation of Shojo-cute which resonate with similar psychological explanations of the visual stimulations that babies use to acquire adult love. Despite often being understood as deeply feminist in its approach to characterisation, Ghibli make liberal use of such representations. Only San the feral wolf-princess heroine of *Princess Mononoke* is remotely transgressive in the way that she is portrayed. Perhaps unsurprisingly she doesn't feature in a recent survey asking men aged 20 thru 40 to rate their favourite Ghibli Girl. Fio Piccolo (*Porco Rosso*) Chihiro (*Spirited Away*), Sheeta (*Laputa: Castle in the Sky,*) Kiki (*Kiki's Delivery Service*) and Nausicaa (*Nausicaa of the Valley of the Wind*) form the top five, all of whom drip with Shojo-Cute. Unsurprisingly, respondents identified a number of key attributes: "I want to protect her like a princess"; "she's cute and girly but cool at the same time"; "she has a cute naivety"; "she has a tomboyish appeal". It might be easy to dismiss these ideas as the perverse voyeuristic utterances of a certain type of male, if they didn't also feature in similar research that considers the way that girls respond to the films.

There is an underlying sub-text of eroticism – even pornography – to some aspects of Japanese Anime, but the Shojo tradition in a Ghibli sense, also offers a commentary on patriarchal society. Men, and particularly women, have established functions in the social order, yet whilst you are a child, anything is possible; so pre-pubescent Kiki can leave home and set up a delivery business in a new town, Nausicaa becomes an eco-warrior, Fio Piccolo is a seaplane engineer. Fantasy lets Ghibli do that, which is of course the point since it allows us to explore in safe and controlled enviroments the things that we can never do or be in real life.

Strangely, Sophie also doesn't appear in the list. Miyazaki is quick to have her claim that she is eighteen and not pretty – although ironically Shojo dictates that she looks barely in her teens and is 'not pretty' in an aspirational Disney Princess kind of way. Similarly wizard Howl borders on the metrosexual – emerald drop earrings, voluminous silk shirts and flamboyant hair. "I see no point in living if I can't be beautiful" he bemoans after Sophie has seen fit to re-organize his bathroom and mix up his hair colours. "It's not that bad, this shade is even better" is Sophie's wise reply. Since the focus of the subtext is the discovery that many expressions of the body can be beautiful, it is really not that surprising that Old Sophie gets all the good lines, and ends up far more appealing than her girlish counterpart.

Sophie (like Elsa) remains unique amongst Ghibli heroines in that her salvation lies in her transformation into a woman. One of the most refreshing aspects of Ghibli is its unashamed celebration of active girlhood. The ability to act independently and to make one's own free choices – often termed 'Agency' - is a recurring theme in Ghibli and a central aspect to the way that it constructs womanhood. One of the frequent readings of the films is as a metaphor for shifts in our society. In Ghibli's heroines we see empowered young women actively engaged in attempts to resolve the problems created by adults; war, environmental damage, discrimination. Sophie reminds us however, that whilst the experiences of girlhood should be trusted and valued, age brings with it new possibilities, hinting at what the other girls may achieve in the future.

Throughout its films, Ghibli presents us with strong, intelligent, independent-minded women. They are also adventurous and active, yet compassionate, communicative, pacifist and virtuous. Their "female" qualities and experiences are often what resolve the crisis at hand and bridge conflicting worlds. Somewhat refreshingly, Sophie is not the only one who needs to come of age. Howl must also learn to conquer his vanity. He is impulsive, with a tendency to run away from his problems; the moving castle of the title, a steampunk inspired cacophony of parts that ambles across the countryside on mechanical legs, acts as a metaphor for his refusal to commit to a purpose. It is through Sophie, that he learns that some things are worth taking a chance on; in much the same way that Belle tames the beast in... um... the Beast.

Like both Belle & the Beast and Elsa & Anna, Howl and Sophie are crossed lovers. It is their relationship – one that takes place between a legitimate and illegitimate body – that lies at the heart of the piece. It is an idea that Miyazaki has explored in a number of his films. In *'Princess Mononoke'*, Prince Ashitaka falls for San the untamed wolf-child; in *'Tales from Earthsea'* Therru, the love interest for hero Arren, reveals herself to be a dragon; Arrietty in the Ghibli retelling of *'The Borrowers'* is a miniature girl who lives in the narrator Sho's dollhouse. This is perhaps where Ghibli's feminist credentials really lie. Akin to third wave feminism itself, like Elsa, the Ghibli heroines tread the contradiction between conformity and transgression. Sophie is challenging in that, in an almost Bridget Jones kind of way, she begins the film with a career as a milliner and eventually finds fulfillment in cooking and cleaning for her man. She is also more confident and in control as her older self. Yet as Old Sophie she offers us validation of an alternate representation of what it means to be beautiful.

Of course, Sophie isn't perfect, nor are most of the other heroines. There is an air of messiness and contradiction that run through not only many of their actions, but how they are visually represented. Yet far from challenging Bettelheim's thesis regarding the role of fairy stories, it re-inforces Ghibli's importance as a mechanism of self-reflection. As third wave feminism suggests, contradiction is in itself a definitive, lived and embodied strategy, as young women's narratives are increasingly becoming diverse, fragmented and embody a 'lived messiness'. Many women, in trying to make sense of this messiness, have turned the focus inward, to the body, and have started from a place where they can exercise a sense of agency. Third wave narratives, like the narratives in Ghibli, or Disney's *Frozen* (perhaps in many fairy tales) describe women's struggles with their identities as well as the contradictory nature of their empowerment. Though Ghibli's visual representations appear to reinforce patriarchal norms by adhering to strict Shojo conventions, these are juxtaposed by less legitimate bodies. As fairy tales, Mayazaki's films offer young women the opportunity to explore their own lived narratives and what it might mean to be beautiful.

References

Synnott, A. (1993) *The Body Social: Symbolism, Self and Society.* London: Routledge.

Butler, J. (1990) *Gender Trouble: Feminism and the Subversion of Identity.* London: Routledge.

Heywood, L. and Drake, J. (1997) 'Introduction', in Heywood, L. and Drake, J. (eds.) *Third Wave Agenda: Being Feminist, Doing Feminism.* Minneapolis: University of Minnesota Press, pp. 1-20.

The voice of educators and education students

Gail Waite

Gail is an experienced youth practitioner and has worked with children, young people and families for over 20 years, predominantly with those considered vulnerable or challenging, in Youth Justice, Social Care and Education. Gail is a lecturer at Brunel and a freelance Restorative Practice trainer and facilitator and has facilitated a number of serious and complex cases, including sexual abuse. She is an accredited restorative practitioner and has recently been researching the application of restorative practice in alternative settings such as digital space and the teaching of restorative practice at undergraduate level.

Stories of 'shame': how can Nathanson's compass of shame help us understand problematic behaviour?

Gail Waite

In this chapter, I will explore how Nathanson's Compass of Shame can support education practitioners to understand challenging and problematic behaviour. In order to fully understand Nathanson's compass of shame, we must first understand something of human motivation. Silvan Tomkins first developed the idea of Affect Theory in the 1960s, by suggesting our environment affects us in nine ways. Tomkins suggests that these affects are distinct and different from emotions and that emotions occur once we become aware of the affect. Seven of these 'affects' can be seen as a continuum, for example interest – excitement (feeling OK – feeling this is the best day ever), distress – anguish, and shame – humiliation and it is these affects that eventually lead to the formation of 'scripts' or patterns of behaviour.

Kelly (2014) argues that we are all intrinsically hard wired with these affects and that we are motivated to maximise positive affect, such as interest – excitement and minimise negative affect such as shame – humiliation.

```
                Enjoyment — Joy
            Interest — Excitement
          Surprise — Startle
        Shame — Humiliation
      Distress — Anguish
         Disgust
      Fear — Terror
    Anger — Rage
   Dissmell
```

Image 1 – Affect Theory Silvan Tomkins

Nathanson developed his Compass of Shame as a way of understanding how individuals react when they become aware of the negative affects mentioned by Tomkins and named the model in this way as shame – humiliation is the first of the negative affects, not as a model for understanding the affect of shame specifically.

When we experience negative feelings triggered by our joy and interest being interrupted, we respond in one of two ways according to Nathanson. We either pay attention to what has caused the affect and 'put it right' or we seek to find other ways of reducing the uncomfortable feelings we are experiencing. Nathanson argues that there are four maladaptive universal systems of defence against the information shame wants us to consider and suggested four libraries of 'scripts' or behaviour patterns that occur when we encounter the shame affect, and 'because he believed pairs of these scripts to be opposites and because they point the way conceptually to negative emotions such as shame that otherwise might remain hidden, he named this construct the *Compass of Shame'* (Kelly 2014, p43) shown below.

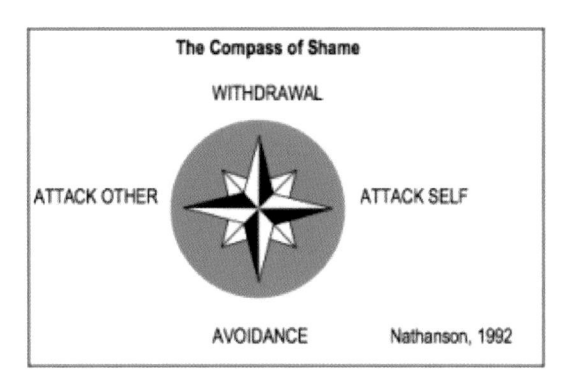

```
The Compass of Shame
        WITHDRAWAL

ATTACK OTHER        ATTACK SELF

        AVOIDANCE        Nathanson, 1992
```

Nathanson, D.L. (1992) Shame and Pride: Affect, sex and the birth of the self

As I mentioned this affect is a continuum, therefore the intensity of the resulting feelings can vary, and result in a range of feelings and emotions being expressed by people, for example embarrassment, hurt, guilt, frustration, stupidity, rejection, powerlessness and shame. How we respond emotionally to the affect of shame is important, 'Braithwaite (1999) suggests the mature and adaptive response is to acknowledge the shame – i.e. to own the offence – and then discharge the shame by taking steps to address the harm caused by the behaviour' (George 2011, np). However, many of us learn ways of managing the difficult feelings of shame in maladaptive ways because they are too painful to acknowledge, these can be understood by looking at Nathanson's *Compass of Shame*.

Emotions that are triggered when we become aware of the shame affect vary and psychological research suggests that individuals are predisposed to either shame-proneness or guilt-proneness and that a predisposition to shame-proneness can lead to negative outcomes such as criminal activity (Tibbets 1997), other risk taking activities and poor mental health (Tagney and Dearing 2002, Tagney et al

2007). Interestingly many people use the feelings of guilt and shame interchangeably, however, it is important to understand that they are fundamentally different 'The majority of shame researchers and clinicians agree that the difference between shame and guilt is best understood as the difference between 'I am bad' (shame) and 'I did something bad' (guilt)' (Brown 2010, p41). What is interesting about this distinction is that feelings of guilt motivate us to find ways to put things right, to return to positive affect and restore relationships whereas feelings of shame are 'associated with attempts to deny, hide or escape the shame-inducing situation' (Tagney and Dearing, 2002, p.8) and result in 'scripts' such as those outlined by Nathanson.

At each pole there are a library of responses or 'scripts' of things to say or do when shame occurs and we don't know how to deal with it. Withdrawal occurs to protect ourselves from others, to prevent further exposure of failure, weakness or judgement. Attack self – is a self-deprecating response to shame, by attacking ourselves we are in control of how much shame we feel. Attack other - is a response in which we seek to transfer the blame onto others and is often demonstrated by aggression, anger or passive-aggressive behaviours. Avoidance is a distraction response, focusing instead on another aspect of self, one that is not flawed. All of these responses, in part, begin to return us to the positive affect state albeit in a maladaptive way, but prevent us from re-establishing connection with people.

Some people navigate the affect of shame successfully, moving from the emotion of shame to guilt and ultimately finding a way to continue with life. Sometimes the intensity and enduring nature of the emotion of shame can result in us becoming 'stuck' in maladaptive responses and learning 'scripts' that are damaging to both ourselves and others. Understanding that what presents on the outside, for example seeking to minimise behaviour (avoidance), become verbally or physically aggressive (attack other) are not necessarily indications that people are not willing or able to take responsibility for their behaviour and any harm caused, merely that they might require some help and support to return to positive affect, 'every violent action is a tragic expression of unmet need'(Rosenberg, 2003, p56) is important. The crucial difference with regards to our response to emotions of shame and guilt is the ability to reflect, 'people experiencing guilt are not challenged to defend the self, but rather are drawn to reflect on their specific behaviour' (George 2011, np).

To illustrate Nathanson's theory I want to share some stories of 'shame'. The first is about a young man I worked with, let's call him Carl. Carl was 14 years old when I first met him, he had a troubled childhood resulting in several foster care placements due to his family circumstances since the age of 5 and was attending a school for children with emotional and behavioural difficulties. The school had a system of behaviour management whereby at the end of each school day children would be given a score in regards to how they had behaved that day, 1 being awful up to 5 being excellent. On the day in question Carl was waiting for his taxi with the other students ready to receive his score. He wasn't expecting a 5 but thought he might have achieved a 3 as he had tried hard to be 'good'. When the teacher came to give Carl his score, he told him it was a 2. As you might imagine his sense of joy and interest was severely interrupted and Carl was unable to manage his feelings of shame and humiliation. He began lashing out at staff, throwing chairs and when his teaching assistant arrived to try to calm the situation he spat in her face. He was very much in 'attack other' according to Nathanson. Eventually the police were called and Carl was excluded from the school for a period of 5 days.

The second story is about a young woman I worked with called Karen. Karen was seen by professionals as a 'problem'. She was 15 when I first met her and hadn't attended mainstream school for a number of years, she was at a specialist school for children with emotional difficulties due to high levels of anxiety, she was self medicating with cannabis, a low level offender and refusing to engage with mental health services or any other support services. One of the first things I remember her Mother telling me when I first arranged to visit her was 'please don't give up on her like everyone else has'. I visited Karen weekly, each week she refused to talk to me about anything significant and each week I would end our hour together by telling her I would see her same day and time next week. This went on for about six weeks, until one day when I made a deal with her, that I would tell her about my life if she would tell me about hers, she agreed. After plotting some details of my life on a kind of road map, I folded the piece of paper, handed it to her and asked her to keep 'my life' safe. We then moved on to her life, she told me about her parents, the domestic abuse her much loved father had subjected her mother to, her having to move away and start again as a result and that she thought she was gay. Karen was deeply ashamed about her father's behaviour, despite loving him very much and was embarrassed and confused that she was attracted to girls. She had 'withdrawn' from many aspects of social life (such as school) and was using cannabis as an 'avoidance' mechanism.

So, what can we learn from Carl and Karen? I believe an understanding of Nathanson's compass of shame has, two key benefits to education professionals. Firstly, it enables us to develop an understanding of human behaviour and how people might react when they have caused harm or in fact been harmed. Secondly, it can help us develop an ethos and framework that helps us support people to move from the potentially painful and damaging emotion of shame to reconnect with individuals, families and societies. The more we put this understanding into practice in our schools, homes and workplaces the better we can enable our children, young people and societies to learn adaptive ways of managing the affect of shame, and the potential for harm to self and others will be reduced. I believe understanding our responses to the affect of shame and the resulting positive or negative emotions can help us change not only our own behaviours but influence those of our society to move from traditional forms of 'justice' and punitive responses to wrong doing to one where individuals do 'the right thing' not from fear of being caught but because they are able to reflect and understand the impact of those behaviours on others, they experience feelings of guilt rather than shame.

References

Brown, B. (2010) *The Gifts of Imperfection: Your Guide to a Wholehearted Life*. Centre City, Minnesota, MN: Hazeldon.

Braithwaite, J. (1997) *Crime, Shame and Reintegration*. Cambridge: Cambridge University Press.

George, G. (2011) *Navigating beyond the compass*. Available at www.rpforschools.net (Accessed 17 February 2016).

Kelly, V. C. and Thorsborne, M. (2014) *The Psychology of Emotion in Restorative Practice*. London: Jessica Kingsley.

Nathanson, D. L. (1992) *Shame and Pride: Affect, Sex and the Birth of The Self*. New York: W. W Norton and Company.

Rosenberg, M. (2003) *Nonviolent Communication: A Language of Life* (2nd edition), Encinitas, CA: Puddle Dancer Press.

Tibbets, S. G. (1997) 'Shame and rational choice in offending decisions', *Criminal Justice Behaviour,* 24, pp. 234 – 255.

Tagney, J. P. and Dearing, R. L. (2002) *Shame and Guilt*. New York:

Guildford Press.

Tagney, J. P., Steuwig, J. and Mashek, D. J. (2007) 'Moral emotions and moral behaviour', *Annual Review of Psychology,* 58, pp. 345-372.

Philip Garner

Professor Philip Garner taught in mainstream and specialist schools for nearly 20 years. Subsequently he joined the staff of the West London Institute prior to its incorporation within Brunel University. Philip has previously held Chairs in Education at Nottingham Trent and Northampton universities. He has undertaken major research projects in Special and Inclusive Education, both within the UK and internationally (including Bhutan, China, Malaysia, Pakistan, Turkey, Oman and Sierra Leone). He has published widely on topics relating to his research interests (including alternative provision for excluded learners, leadership and change in education communities and teacher development).

The voice of educators and education students

Circling the Cairo cement works and dented Dodges: a tale of daring and survival

Philip Garner

This somewhat heartfelt account is taken from my research diary – maintained throughout a major part of my nearly 50 years in education. I have chosen it because it captures the sometimes chaotic life that we lead well beyond the scheduled professional activity that draws us to locations across the globe. I loved being in Cairo, for its life, its people, its lack of traffic lights. As with every other academic visit I've made, I came away the winner – learning so much about myself, a previously unknown education system and a newly acquired respect for a city's drivers. This was not the ideal location to test out the now standard RAG-rating evaluation process of a teaching programme: the city is fabled as only having 9 traffic lights in its entire metropolitan area. My helter-skelter daily journey around its universities as part of a recent Erasmus+ project became a topic to which my shaking diary-hand returned on repeated occasions. As a tyro researcher in my early years at Brunel, it was never explained that these nerve-shredding moments were, in fact, part of the researchers lot.

The taxi, ordered by badgering at first - then haranguing - the stubbly cast-off from the set of a spaghetti western in the lobby, took an age to come. It thus seemed such a timely, remedial suggestion from the slightly unctuous and terribly eager young Egyptian receptionist on the front desk of the Holiday Inn. Ah yes, that bastion of security for the timid and forlorn, dripping in marble like a poor man's *Porcenalosa*. The aforesaid maiden, coiffured and mannered, in the style of a courtesan, offered the limousine ride, courtesy of the hotel. The egotist in me ran out a clear winner, as the impulse to act like a colonial dick took firm hold.

'Limousine' is a loose approximation for the 9-year old Prius that duly creaked through the fortified gate, accompanied by the routine inspection of the boot (or trunk: we are after all on Holiday Inn property now) by militia who were suitably tooled-up to commit half of Cairo to an orgasm of cordite. No stray IS infiltrator being found, the heaving Toyota was sent on its way, coughing up the ramp and subsiding with a protest at my feet.

To my consternation, the chauffeur was also a quick-change artist: none other than the Lee van Cleef character from the lobby. A nifty change of cap and an equally deft polish of near citrus-coloured teeth allowed him to double as a driver. My luck was in; at least I felt that he would not risk his dual income by going about his business as a faded anti-hero from the Paris-Dakar rally.

Wrong. I was at least reassured in the knowledge that I'd had a scrub and change of clothes – terrified skid marks on boxers are a car crash victim's penultimate indignity, preceding the insertion of a catheter by a usually smug nurse, who appears to enjoy that part of her job just a little too much. I was correspondingly right to be assured of my attire.

I've never been so keen to die quickly, such was the rank and searing terror that coursed through me in the 50-minute ride. An automobile game of pinball, the machine itself being a dusty street-map of inner-urban Cairo called Maadi. They should strip two vowels and call it mad. As yet another Dodge pick-up careered towards me, like a mechanical limbo dancer on acid, I started to pray. Would I ever see my lovely family again? Would I see the hills, climb on grey, scented volcanic effluent in the Lakes? All life passed before me, as rag-tag drivers, sounding horns like a frantic requiem for an academic life gone bad, veered this way and that. Manic, noisy and full of the smell of sweat and fear – and probably the early warnings of tell-tale streaks in my Primark underpants. And we had yet to arrive at the cement works, the very mention of which brings a curdled, hysterical laugh to the face of seasoned Cairo cab drivers.

"Here! Here!". Van Cleef's triumphal shout announced our arrival. Or was it a question? Either way, I cowered, sweating like an abattoir-bound hog, decoding the circumstances that had led me to this. Was it my stubborn, Putinesque insistence that I curry the favour of others by creating a version of Mr Can Do? Or a latent death-wish, which seems to surface whenever I visit Africa – last witnessed in my chaotic, diarrhoea-ridden retreat from Tangier, when the last exit promised by departing this earth became the only focus in my line of sight.

This was similar. The Eisenstein-style industrial complex that I had arrived at exuded menace, with its malevolent columns, pipes and gantries. And I was trapped. Even more so now that the Cairo cowboy had left the Prius, door wide open, to seek direction from Captain Concrete, deeper within the factory. That door became the necessary invitation to the local youth to chance their arm, closing in on the pallid and haunted captive in the car. Six, seven…perhaps more…pairs of inquisitive eyes entered my space, barely inches

The voice of educators and education students

from my face, smelling their fearful prey like a seasoned pack of hyena from the continent's arid plains to the south.

A north English accent, a fall-back weapon, usefully deployed alongside pleading mention of 'Bobby Charlton' and 'David Beckham', was aimlessly and in blunderbuss fashion directed at these interlopers. An immediate and telling response, 'Manchester, Manchester, Mister?' told me that I had scored with these youthful Cairenes. A small victory, away from home. Three points.

But I was soon ejected, summarily so, from a new sense of security. Van Cleef was back, Niagara-sweat pouring from his brows to stain his faded blue chauffeur-shirt. His thinly disguised scowl broadcast his frustration. After all, he was Mr Cairo, born and bred; this was his manor, he's the geezer round these parts. More cowering from the non-paying passenger, followed by a lurch at Mach 1.3 towards the cement work's perimeter, donkey-drawn carts of plastic waste scattered as we went. An exit, however fraught with underpant-soiling terror it was to be, was in sight.

Cleefy (for we now had become friends of sorts, locked in this auto-nightmare courtesy of the perfect storm of a Prius that had just one (high) speed, a road network which induced psychotic driver behaviour, and an abiding love of cement) grinned fanatically. He, like me, knew the exit strategy.

The Japanese motor protested noisily and, as a scented clutch-mist invaded my nostrils, our metal coffin ejaculated onto the gloriously named Cornishe, the boulevard along the Nile. We were free. Free to join the mayhem and adrenalin rush of crumpled Corollas, dented Dodges and fragmented Fords on the journey to the suburban south. Cleefy high-fived, and belched an audible approval of his map-reading skill. The lost 35 minutes, the cement-works saga, was deleted from his cache. He was, again, the main man; he assumed a familiar gunslinger swagger to accompany the mood.

Setting me down at the University was a celebration. Egyptian marching bands played waltzing pharaoh sounds, and Cleefy was sufficiently invigorated by the rediscovery of his capacity to drive on a roadway rather than a pavement that he made an introduction himself to the University Rector. In the coming months, no doubt at all, he will be inaugurated as the Ennio Morricone Chair of Psychotic Driving at Helwan University.

I lived to fight another day, of course, most recently reprising my Cairo experiences by jousting with the rip-off Honda scooters that choke downtown Lahore. Who needs the excitement of the null hypothesis when transit offers such terrors?

Christopher Ince

Christopher is a Lecturer in Education at Brunel University London. He holds a Doctorate in Education, Postgraduate Certificate in Education and Bachelor's degree in Physics and Astrophysics from the University of Sheffield. He was a Science teacher and Head of Physics for ten years in UK secondary schools. The majority of his academic work and research is focused on STEM Education, Policy Analysis, and Curriculum Reform; particularly examining the power structures and discourses revealed during educational 'turning points'.

Quack: a reflection on teaching science in a UK secondary school

Christopher Ince

Being a teacher, there are many wonderful things that happen during any given school-day. There are some less than wonderful days, but working with teenagers can be so much more positive than many people think; a public perception that could be caused by many factors.

Every now and again, something happens that I feel is worth sharing, simply because I like to show people how great it can be to be a teacher. In my teaching career there have been many: informing a Y7 class that we were learning about menstruation, only to be immediately asked by a precocious young gentleman if that was why I was wearing a bright red shirt; having to explain to a Y11 student that it was "impolite" to use the Cruciatus Curse on a fellow student who got in his way (and technically worth a spell in Azkaban); being told that I looked "like Captain America" only for the student to add "at the start of the film…when he was all skinny"; I could go on, and on.

But, if you might indulge me in a little Physics:

The voice of educators and education students

It's first lesson of the day, a lesson on gravitational force with a Y10 class (set two). The class have carried out the experimental activity, disproved Aristotle with a piece of paper and some paperclips and then have been set some problems to attempt.

"Sir, what speed would a duckdo fall at?"

At this point I wasn't quite paying attention.

"I don't know, how high is it above the ground?"
"About 24 metres."
"Have you already worked out its gravitational energy?"
"No."
"If you know that then you can set it equal to the kinetic energy and derive an approximate velocity. Have you already cancelled out the masses on both sides?"
"No."
"Well what's the mass of this..."
"Duckdo."

It was at this point that I realised that I was missing something. The hubbub of the classroom meant I hadn't heard the end of his initial question, but it was no clearer to me now.

"Duckdo?"
"Yes."

He grinned at me. That sort of a grin that you know when hijinks are afoot.

"Right. Well what's the mass of this...duckdo?"

"About 200g."
"From 24m?"
"Yup."

He grinned again and confusion at what was going on again registered in my brain. I glanced at his friends who were sat on his left, quietly watching, grins on *their* faces. I picked up a pen and turned to the board.

"Well you can assume that all of the gravitational energy, mass multiplied by gravitational field strength multiplied by the vertical height above the ground, is converted into kinetic energy; the m, 0.2kg, is on both sides and so cancels. The only factor is the 24m."

I finished the problem and wrote the answer on the board, he looked disappointed. I sat down behind my desk and turned to the girls on his right.

"Is something going on that I don't know about?"
"I dunno"

I glanced back at the boys.

"Is this some sort of trick? I've never heard of this. Are we seriously calculating the velocity of duck faeces?"

I looked back to the girls.

"Have you heard of a duckdo?"

They shook their heads and one of them turned to the instigator of this:

"What's a duckdo?"

"QUACK!"

--

Incidentally, not accounting for air resistance or other energy losses, it would have hit the ground at approximately 22 metres per second.

$$\text{Kinetic Energy} = \text{Gravitational Potential Energy}$$

$$\frac{m \times v^2}{2} = m \times g \times h$$

$$\frac{v^2}{2} = g \times h$$

$$v^2 = 2(g \times h)$$

$$v = \sqrt{2(g \times h)}$$

$$v = \sqrt{2(9.81 \times 24)}$$

$$v \approx 21.7 \text{ ms}^{-1}$$

The voice of educators and education students

Kate Hoskins

Kate Hoskins is a Reader in Education at Brunel University. Her research focuses on education policy, identity and inequalities in relation to further and higher education opportunities and experiences. Her most recent publication, STEM, Social Mobility and Equality: Avenues for Widening Access, examines the role of the family in intra- and inter-generational social movement. She takes a genealogical approach to researching social mobility, using a university chemistry department as a case study to explore participants' motives for pursuing a STEM undergraduate degree and the influences that have shaped them.

Theorising 'success'

Kate Hoskins

Get dressed, get blessed. Try to be a success (Bob Dylan, 1965)

Introduction

The purpose of this short piece is to examine literature exploring the concept of 'success'. Drawing on my research examining how female professors construct their career success, the aim is to highlight the contested nature of what constitutes 'success', and to consider how this knowledge could be drawn on by policy-makers to better inform attempts to improve academic outcomes for all children, regardless of their background.

I concur with Bradford and Hey (2007: 26) who argue that 'discourses of success mesh with other discursive fields and sites of identity and belonging'. Success in contemporary western societies, whether characterized as a continuum, a road or a series of moments of ever more complex accomplishments or events has several key dimensions that might operate either individually or collectively within a particular context. Key dimensions, or levers, of success include (i) aptitude (Kristoff, 2009); (ii) executive function (Carey, 2008); (iii) propensity for hard work (Brooks, 2009); (iv) luck (Gladwell, 2008); (v) serendipity (Prestine, 2009); (vi) social patterns and culture (Gladwell, 2008), and (vii) circumstantial factors (including historical context) (Gladwell, 2008). I now take each of these dimensions in turn.

Turning first to (i) aptitude, Kristoff (2009: 2) has argued that:

While I.Q. doesn't measure pure intellect — we're not certain exactly what it does measure — differences do matter, and a higher I.Q. correlates to greater success in life.

Higher I.Q. (however contentious) might facilitate success because, for example, of the increased possibilities for gaining formal qualifications and subsequent higher status and better rewarded employment. Indeed, doing well academically in school also takes its place alongside luck, hard work and creativity as a further ingredient of success for my cohort. All of the five women interviewed for my Masters research (Hoskins, 2007), who were all educated in the 1950s, reported that they were 'good' at school in terms of being academically able and consequently spent the majority, if not all, of their school lives in the top sets. Academic ability was an attribute highly valued by 1950s grammar schools, particularly 'traditional grammar schools […] with [their] single–minded pursuit of success in exams' (Evans, 1991: 40). Yet arguably aptitude alone will not ensure success – whilst my earlier research found it to be a lever of success, it was coupled with luck and hard work (Hoskins, 2007).

Carey (2008: 1) has suggested that a more significant ingredient of success is what he terms (ii) executive function which involves three key skills: first, 'the ability to resist distractions or delay gratification to finish a job'; second, it involves 'working memory, the capacity to hold and manipulate multiple numbers or ideas in the mind'; and third, what he explains as the 'cognitive flexibility, the ability to appreciate another person's point of view and to adapt when demands change'. Carey (2008: 1) claims that executive function 'is more strongly associated with school success than I.Q.'; success, it seems, breeds success.

However, Brooks (2009) has argued that (iii) propensity for hard work may trump aptitude, executive function and even talent when it comes to understanding success. According to Brooks (2009: 1):

The key factor separating geniuses from the merely accomplished is not a divine spark. It's not I.Q., a generally bad predictor of success even in realms like chess. Instead, it's deliberate practice. Top performers spend more hours (many more hours) rigorously practicing their craft.

Similarly Gladwell (2008: 39, italics as original) has suggested that the 'people at the very top don't work harder or even much harder than everyone else. They work much, *much* harder'. Gladwell (2008) invokes what he calls the 10,000 hour rule, which is described as being the magic number of hours that an individual needs to build up in a particular area, for example, computer programming, in order to achieve expertise; but arguably working long hours alone will not guarantee success.

It seems that (iv) luck and serendipity might also play a part. According to Gladwell (2008), luck is also required for career success. That is, being in the right place at the right time and taking lucky breaks as they present themselves. I found that luck was perceived to be one of the most important ingredients in the respondents' perceptions and constructions of their career success – but this is problematic, as some women are inclined to play down more 'assertive' behaviours like careerism, managerialism and power (Hoskins, 2010).

A further, and related, lever of success might be (v) serendipity (Prestine, 2009), that is some success may be attributable to elements of chance, destiny and/or accident. My doctoral research found that 5 of the 20 respondents interviewed accounted for some aspects of their academic career success as serendipitous and due to being in the right place at the right time. According to Prestine (2009: 115), an academic woman reflecting on her career experiences:

> *As I now reflect on it, it seems to me that my career path has been characterized to a large extent by chance, fate, serendipity, or what you will, rather than cool calculation or careful plotting. I have watched others carefully calculate what needs to be done [...] to gain prominence, identify, and then ally themselves with what topics are 'hot,' and plot their moves from position to position and university to university. That is simply not me.*

Yet combinations of hard work, luck, aptitude and/or serendipity are not necessarily enough to ensure a successful academic career. Some female academics with aptitude do not become 'successful' in terms of achieving occupational promotion (Hoskins, 2014). So, what of the role of social and cultural patterns in achieving success?

Gladwell (2008: 105) argues that the very successful, the 'outlier', benefits from (vi) social patterns and culture that 'interlock to form a culture of achievement'. Gladwell (2008: 54) cites the example of Bill Gates' success evoking luck and social patterns to account for his achievements, arguing that 'he was lucky enough to go to a private school with its own computer at the dawn of the information revolution'. This raises a question - what role is played by the 'fixed' elements of success, i.e. an individual's cultural background and circumstance (e.g. family background and the historical moment an individual is born into)?

A significant tenet of Gladwell's (2008) argument is his assertion that the final factor, (vii) culture and history, will significantly shape an individual's possibilities for success. Brooks (2009: 1) has argued that 'exceptionally successful people are not lone pioneers who created their own success'. Rather, success, according to Brooks (2009) is seen as mediated by a combination of levers including an individual's I.Q., environment, attitude to work and ability to convert 'lucky' breaks. In sum:

Genius does find a way of rising to the surface. Culture, zeitgeist, family, genes, history and chance help carry it along (Halpern, 2009: 5).

There is, perhaps, a critical tension between 'individualised' accounts of success and 'sociologically' inflected accounts of how, why and what success is.

In my view we need to view success relationally, that is, in particular situated contexts, as one way of beginning to understand it. Indeed, whilst exploring academic literature examining career success, as well as mainstream, management and popular psychological literature on career success, I was struck by its contextual and historically-specific nature; success means different things to different people at different moments in time. What an individual or institution might have constituted as a success previously, may no longer count because of shifting parameters and changing conceptualisations - and that has never been more apparent than in the current COVID-19 pandemic. Thus, as a conceptual starting point, two aspects of success might be the ways in which it is historically specific and socially constructed and the ways in which it is inextricably linked to the context in which it is sought and achieved (thus contingent) and is consistent with an individual's habitus (Bourdieu, 1977).

A further consideration of success relates to its attributes; success can be viewed as an unfolding and continuous process, a story that is told over periods of time. As such, success is frequently conceptualised in popular psychology as a road to be travelled, a journey with the promise, ultimately, of arriving at a destination with the realisation of achievement (Leatz, 1993). Success is characterised as the fulfilment of individual goals. Success has also been understood as a continuum as in Jones' (2004) *Success Continuum*, a popular psychology book, which 'shares the secrets' of the immensely successful (e.g. Bill Gates). Jones (2004: 14) argues that success is:

> *Not a destination... it is an ongoing process; what you achieve today builds off of successes you have had in the past and of lessons from your failures; luck may present an opportunity; you must take action to realise success.*

Yet in mainstream, management literature that explores occupational success (see for example Kossek and Lambert 2005), the notion of a ladder, characterized by achieving a series of goals or meeting certain criteria, is a recurring metaphor for conceptualising what success *should* mean to individuals and institutions (both private and public sector institutions). In my view, encouraging employees to view their employment success as a ladder is arguably a useful way for employers to maintain staff engagement, but not always of great benefit to the individual staff member.

If success is contextual, historical and inscribed by habitus, the current education system emphasis on academic attainment in England is mis-placed. For many students, academic success as it is constructed by policy-makers is not the measure of success that applies or is relevant to their aspirations and personal circumstances (Hoskins and Barker, 2016: 2020). A broader view of success is needed that takes account of the ways in which success is constructed in both subjective and objective ways. In my research with 20 female professors from working- and middle-class backgrounds to understand how they constructed career success, all of the respondents, but especially those from working-class families, had felt that they were not worthy of their career success. They had felt like frauds, interlopers at both grammar school and whilst working in the academy. Yet I kept pondering that these women are undeniably successful, so why do they construct themselves in self-deprecating ways? Perhaps these women, similarly to Reay (1997: 27), are engaged in a process of:

Reconciling what I have become with what I was, while simultaneously trying to carve out a self that I can feel at ease with.

Perhaps as educators this process of finding ways to fit, when socio-culturally we might feel we stand out, is an important area of focus that we need to engage with to really help our students achieve success in their future lives?

Bibliography

Bourdieu, P. (1977) *Outline of a Theory of Practice*. Cambridge: Cambridge University Press.

Bradford, S., Hey, V. (2007) 'Successful subjectivities? The successification of class, ethnic and gender positions', *Journal of Education*

Policy, 22(6), pp. 595-614.

Carey, B. (2008) *Training young brains to behave*. The New York Times.

Evans, M. (1991) *A Good School: Life at a Girls' Grammar School in the 1950s*. London: The Women's Press Limited.

Gladwell, M. (2008) *Outliers*. USA: Hachette Book Group.

Halpern, S. (2009) 'Making It', *The New York Review of Books*. Vol. 56, No.9.

Hoskins, K. and Barker, B. (2020) *STEM, Social Mobility and Equality: Avenues for Widening Access*. Hampshire: Palgrave MacMillan.

Hoskins, K. and Barker, B. (2016) 'Aspirations and young people's constructions of their futures: investigating social mobility and social reproduction', *British Journal of Educational Studies*, 65(1), pp. 45 – 67

Hoskins, K. (2007) '*A classed and gendered exploration of success*'. Paper given at Gender and Education Association (GEA) Conference, Trinity College Dublin, March 2007.

Jones, J. (2004) *The Success Continuum*. Illinois: Xlibris Corporation.

Kossek, E. E. and Lambert, S. J. (2005) *Work and Life Integration: Organizational, Cultural, and Individual Perspectives*. New York: Routledge.

Kristoff, N. (2009) *How to raise our I.Q.* The New York Times.

Leatz, C. A. (1993) *Career Success/Personal Stress*. London: McGraw-Hill Inc.

Prestine, N. A. (2009) 'The accidental professor', in Mertz, N. T. (ed) (2009) *Breaking into the All-Male Club*. Albany. State University of New York Press, pp. 115-124.

Reay, D. (1997) 'The double-bind of the 'working class' feminist academic: the success of failure of the failure of success?', in Mahony, P. and Zmroczek, C. (1997) (Eds) *Class Matters:'Working Class' Women's Perspectives on Social Class*. London. Taylor & Francis, pp. 18-29.

Lewis Fogarty

I currently lecture on the MA in Education programme at Brunel, responsible primarily for the leadership and management specialist pathway. This role is informed by my other responsibility as Director of an Early Education and Childcare company based in Windsor. As well as considering myself a teacher, I am also a student at the thesis stage of my EdD here at Brunel, focusing on leadership in the Early Years, forming a bridge between my responsibilities.

The voice of educators and education students

Advocating for education and care in equal measure throughout education

Lewis Fogarty

Over the past decade I have been involved with education at all levels, from early years children at 9 months old to adults on Master's programmes. This experience has stemmed from an unshakeable habit of not leaving my own places of education. For instance, I have moved from a student at secondary school to Teacher and now a hirer of two unused classrooms for my Early Education company. Similarly, I have transitioned from my BSc in Psychology to MA in Education through to my ongoing EdD at Brunel University, in parallel to my recently appointed position as Lecturer on the MA programme. This range of experience has been very powerful and has motivated me to write this paper.

The purpose of this paper is to explicate an emerging idea from my reflections on my experience that has led me to believe that an essential ingredient of educational prosperity is for all teachers to embed care and education in equal measure, in their practice. It is also essential that at every stage of education, from early years to higher education, we all consider ourselves teachers. Furthermore, as Miller (2018) states, teachers are the lifeblood of an education system and without them objectives for society as a whole may not be realised. I hope that this paper will challenge the reader to reflect on their role as a teacher and to consider how embedded care and education are in their daily practice.

For clarity, by care I mean to actively consider a learner's physiological needs, that they feel safe with a sense of connection to others and know that they are respected as an individual. For my understanding of education, I draw on the work of Biesta (2015) who offers three domains of educational purpose that include qualification which is to do with the transmission and acquisition knowledge and skills, socialisation that refers to the importance of initiating learners into cultural, religious and professional traditions. Finally, subjectification, which refers to the importance of learners becoming empowered and responsible individuals. I am concerned that currently in education there is a much narrower understanding of what education is. This is captured by John Hattie stating that 'although there is more to education than academic achievement, in the end, this is what is supposed to matter most' (Hattie, 2008, p. 245–255).

Building on this concern, I would like to now offer you how I see the current education landscape, broadly speaking. Whilst you may disagree with this pertaining to your own practice, I would encourage you to think broadly of education at this stage, as the time for introspection will shortly follow. I would like to propose that typically at each stage of education the focus is as follows: 90% care and 10% education in early years, 70% care and 30% education in primary, 50% care and 50% education in secondary school until GCSE years where it becomes 30% care and 70% education and finally in higher education where it is 90% education and 10% care. Many readers may find themselves conflicted in their broad agreement with this, but the reality is that they are under pressure from the 'terrors of performativity' (Ball, 2003). This reality is becoming increasingly hostile and troubling with the unabating funding crisis and narrow sense of purpose that perpetuates.

There is much more to say around these speculative percentages, for example what if the primary school did SATS in year 2? Also, considering that pastoral work in secondary schools could often be left to non-teaching individuals. In reality, is care even more marginalised in a teacher's gaze? These numbers are intended to be thought-provoking, if you find them unpalatable I would ask you instead to consider the unavoidable and uncomfortable truth that there are times, at every stage of education, where care is marginalised to ensure education (in a narrow sense) remains at the forefront, even increasingly in early years.

In spite of these difficulties, it is essential as teachers we strive to persevere and offer education and care in equal measure at all stages of education. This is to promote learner well-being above all else and to ensure our learners are happy, because if students aren't happy, they are not engaged and if they aren't engaged then they aren't learning. Moreover, particularly as learners progress through the education system, towards more independent study, they can naturally feel more alone and also under more pressure. Lewis (2019) reported that UK universities are in the middle of a mental health crisis and that there has been a six-fold increase in children and young people's mental health issues since 1995. Also, suicide is the leading cause of death between the ages of 20 and 34. Drawing on my experience, in relation to these statistics, compels me to suggest that a stronger presence of care throughout the education system would help reduce these painful statistics.

I would therefore like to spend the rest of this paper offering a framework to approach education that lends itself to a more appropriate focus on both education and care at all levels. You are the expert at your level of education so consider now the time for introspection. This framework is in the form of four pillars of pedagogy that I not only promote, but practice. This is the pedagogical framework enacted in my nursery, Always Growing, and has become embedded in all the teacher's vocabulary and practice through their individual induction and development. This is part of their learning journey and they are encouraged to act with agency at all times within this framework, as should any teacher when offered a framework of any kind.

Relationships are essential at all levels of education, between all stakeholders. If these relationships are reassuring, then individuals will be more willing to take risks or ask for help and to share ideas more. This promotes care because the relationships are first and foremost about listening, establish trust and supporting one another to feel welcome and happy. As previously mentioned, if learners are not happy they will not be engaged or learning, which is integral to education of course. Therefore, reassuring relationships is the first pillar and the heartbeat of our pedagogy.

Clear communication is the second pillar and is about more than meaningful pedagogical conversations to support the teaching and learning in our setting. Whilst these are important and recognise the power of language to make learning engaging and inevitable, this would be to focus solely on education. A focus should also be around building on reassuring relationships by listening to each other and reacting in a thoughtful and reassuring way. Through communicating clearly, stronger reassuring relationships can be formed.

By having reassuring relationships throughout organisations and communicating clearly and thoughtfully, individuals, be it children, adults or parents, will feel more cared for. These conversations will then spark continuous curiosity, which is our third pillar, that not only promotes individuals to get to know more about others in their learning environment, but also to be curious about their own development, and encourage them to flourish in their own unique way. The combination of foci of curiosity lends itself perfectly to embedding care and education in equal measure in teachers' everyday practice.

All the previous pillars are encouraged and sustained by the educational environment and this needs to be an enabling environment which is our fourth pillar. This is more than what you can see in a classroom or lecture theatre. It is what you can hear, taste smell and feel too and inclusivity is essential. In an enabling environment where inclusion is embedded, all children can feel cared for and supported. From here, they can go on to be curious about exploring this environment with their friends and teachers, making learning and development inevitable.

This pedagogical framework encompasses so many widely regarded approaches to pedagogy, however this broadness is also a vulnerability, where the focus can be distracted from a balance between education and care, particularly in the current educational milieu. It is therefore easy to overlook the nuances that surround each pillar, but it is not acceptable for teachers to acquiesce in the face of the 'terrors of performativity' (Ball, 2003). Instead, teachers must recognise the imperative of forming reassuring relationships with all stakeholders, communicating clearly with them to fuel continuous curiosity and ensure this occurs within an environment that is enabling for all.

As teachers, we need to stay true to these imperatives in offering care and education from the early years through to higher education in equal measure. In doing so, we can ensure our learners are experiencing education in the broadest sense of qualification, socialisation and subjectification. From my experiences throughout all stages of education, I see this in many educational settings, but perhaps at the price of teacher well-being. Therefore, until there are significant shifts in policy contexts, care may well continue to be marginalised and seen as something in addition to education, rather than being in an essential antecedent for it.

References

Ball, S. (2003) 'The teacher's soul and the terrors of performativity', *Journal of Education Policy*, 18(1), pp. 215–228.

Biesta, G. (2015) 'What is education for? On good education, teacher judgement, and educational professionalism', *European Journal of Education*, 50 (1), pp. 75-87.

Hattie, J. (2008) *Visible Learning*. London/New York: Routledge.

Lewis, A. (2019) *Universities shouldn't just treat mental illness – they should help prevent it too*. Available at: https://mosaicscience.com/story/universities-shouldnt-just-treat-mental-illness-they-should-help-prevent-it-too-SLU-CBT-depression-student-anxiety (Accessed: 19 February 2020).

Miller, P. (2018) *The Nature of School Leadership: Global Practice Perspectives*. London: Palgrave Macmillan.

The voice of educators and education students

Antoine J Rogers

Dr Antoine J Rogers, Codirects Brunel's Urban Scholars Progrmme; an educational intervention for young people to promote widening participation in HE and sustained engagement with learning. A Higher Education Academy (HEA) Senior Fellow, his pedagogical approach has been recognised as effective in raising students aspirations and particularly those from underrepresented groups.

A diasporic response to Black Lives Matter

Spaces of Protests:
White Fragility and Racial Fatigue

Antoine J Rogers

Toni Morrison identified her struggle to embrace 'Black Is Beautiful', the slogan that emerged in the 1970s. Morrison understood the mantra's popularity and emergence as a social political tool of the Black Power Movement of the time. Black WAS beautiful, and Morrison questioned why the statement needed to be said. When I arrived at a Black Lives Matter (the demo and the broad political movement) I felt a similar conundrum; holding a measure of discomfort with the need to say Black Lives Matter with a measure of trepidation in my ability to verbally articulate what should be universally understood. Of course, Black Lives Matter.

In my native Chicago I joined demos to protest police brutality beginning in 1991 with demos against the senseless beating of Rodney King by Los Angeles cops. Later I joined a political group 'Queer to the Left' to help bring attention to race and class issues in LGBT communities. Into my 20s, before moving to the UK, demos became spaces to not only protest; they were locations of connection and engagement with others, where 'I' became 'WE' to make a collective registration of discontent and anger.

Over 20 years living in the UK, my connection to spaces of protest changed. At anti-war demos before Bush's invasion of Iraq; or even at more recent demos directed at Trump, as a Black American, I became more aware yet not distracted by the predominance of white people in these spaces of protest. I continued to connect through a universal protest and a universal(ish) narrative of No War.

The week following George Floyd's death, I decided not to attend most Black Live Matter domos that took place. On demos, I expect to have conversations with strangers: conversations about our intention for being in the space, and frequent conversations about a shared collective purpose. Spaces of protest are spaces of learning or they should be. Nevertheless, I was unsure how to negotiate anticipated conversations with white people; conversations that require an emotional capacity to do work; work required when/if one accommodates for another person's learning and processing. I did not think I could do this work at a Black Lives Matter demonstration in spaces of protest as British as Hyde Park and Parliament.

With protest aims so layered and complicated, as layered and complicated as the statement 'Black Lives Matter' itself, I thought the demo focused on the American Embassy seemed safe - politically and emotionally. The crowd was dense and as I stood in a **black political** space, I quickly felt how it was not a **physical** Black space. Outnumbered by white people, I was distracted and overwhelmed by the multiple ways white people held the space.

Based on overheard conversations, I surmised some white people were newly 'woke', able to see, perhaps event accept the argument that inherent privileges come with whiteness. Near me and seemingly everywhere that day, was a large presence of young white men who occupied the space differently; and with a confident swagger that seemed arrogant. Some of them had cameras. They took pictures of me without permission and did so in locations above me. White men stood above me and pointed their camera at me. Their occupation of a Black political space unsettled me. Hearing them yell Black Lives Matter amplified unsettled feelings or, how the kids say it, they 'triggered' me.

Some white people lead the crowd in the call/response, a fundamental unifying element of every demo, rally, and march. I felt particularly unsettled when white people led the chant 'NO JUSTICE /NO PEACE'; and more so when white people yelled 'SAY HIS NAME/GEORGE FLOYD.' Then the crowd yelled out an unexpected new slogan at least new to me; 'BLACK SKIN IS NOT A CRIME.' Hearing this, I stood verbally paralyzed. I was unable to form my lips around those words. I was also unable to name what I felt. Eventually a Black woman turned to me and said, 'I'm not responding to white people leading THAT call.' Paralyzed no more. YES! I yelled.

In London, on the approach to the Embassy, there was no social distancing and not much organisation. With no effort I clearly heard conversations of people around me. There was no space to process the complexity of the situation with people who were part of my group. Aware that if I engaged in a conversation, other white people would hear me. Risky work is required to hold white people's engagement with racialized politics and especially risky without knowing if/when a white person experiences a moment(s) of clarity that contributes to an awareness and understanding of white privilege. The work required to accommodate a white person's process of knowing and understanding can be risky because it can lead to what writers call racial fatigue. This work can be especially risky without knowing if work has been done since those moments of clarity.

The voice of educators and education students

Over time in work and social spaces, Black people gain an increased awareness of white fragility; and the potential consequences if one triggers, offends or makes white people feel uncomfortable about race - theirs/yours. Many white people around me asserted their allyship without asking me if I wanted it. A component of Black survival is the ability to negotiate (at times carefully) around white fragility. To do so is especially challenging when white people assert their allyship on matters of race along with the intitled assumption that being an ally is of mutual benefit; and should be welcomed. White privilege in operation, to not ask if allyship is wanted, or to critically interrogate the self to assess if enough work has been done to be a mutually beneficial ally.

On the approach to the Embassy I witnessed a range of ways Black people accommodated for white people's learning and processing. But a concern derives from my awareness of the potentially exhausting work to accommodate white people who seemed to have not done the work; any work; other than showing up with a sign. I wondered if young Black people considered and scrutinized their own capacity to accommodate. How much space had they allotted for their own processes and processing to avoid the draining effects of racial fatigue? Overhearing some conversations, I wanted to offer young Black protestors words of caution given to me years ago by a Black American feminist/activist friend.

"To guard their precious intellectual and psychic energies; and to not cast their precious pearls before the wilfully ignorant who masquerade as allies. That they may be friends/acquaintances may give a false hope that a desire to UNDERSTAND is mutual when what is going on is spiritual vampirism."

I am also challenged by what is at times a disproportionate focus on the Black American experience above other Black African Diasporic experiences in the West. There is a risk of amplifying what goes on in the USA over and above what has happened/is happening in the UK and elsewhere in the Western Black Diaspora. At the Embassy, protesters held the Black Lives Matter narrative without a collective ability to specify the narrative to a UK context. In naming those killed by the police, Black American deaths were disproportionately represented: Trevon Martin; Breanna Taylor and obviously George Floyd. Interestingly the crowd called out Stephen Lawrence's name a few times; but Mark Duggan's name was called out just once.

Throughout the West there has been a long war on Black people which is why the Western Black Diaspora responded to the death of George Floyd. Still across the Diaspora, Black people must work to articulate specific demands to their respective governments and societies; and by societies, I mean the white majorities in their respective countries. Within this work, Black people must be aware of the need to avoid and negotiate around encounters of white fragility: "to guard their precious intellectual and psychic energies". The powers that be' and among them especially white people with historical and contemporary racialized privileges throughout the West; do not deflect to the USA. 'Use this opportunity to get your own dirty house in order (to quote a Black British feminist friend).'Reflect on your history; your privileges and your fragility; DO THE WORK/YOUR WORK. But importantly, until you do YOUR work, please leave Black folks out of it. This is what an ally looks like.

The voice of educators and education students

Wendy King

I am the STEM programme coordinator and ITE lecturer in chemistry and science at Brunel. Prior to this, I worked as the Head of Science in a challenging all through school in Stratford. My interests are in integrated STEM learning, and providing teachers with skills to deliver this effectively.

The voice of educators and education students

Conversations with students

Wendy King

'Ah minge off Miss'
'But your BTEC work, when are you going to get it in for marking?'

'Keys, Jack'
'I didn't steal your keys!'
'I didn't tell you my keys were stolen.'
'Yeah, but I didn't steal them.'

'Hey George, how are you today? What are you doing out here on your own? Everything ok, you look nervous.'
'I'm going to ask a girl out. My heart is pounding and my stomach is churning.'
'Well it's pretty normal to feel that when you're about to ask someone out, it's a brave move to put yourself out there.'
'I don't know, I think it might be my Crohn's disease.'

'I want to work for Dyson, I like vacuums.'
'Great, so how does an ionic bond form?'

'Can we tape our mouths shut?'
'Please do.'

'Sam, you ok? What's upset you so much?'
Blub, blub, snot, snot.
'Sam, please talk to me.'
'James and Gavin...' blub, blub, snot, snot
'What did James and Gavin do?'
'They told me....' Blub, blub, snot, snot....'I had a girlfriend!'
Waaaaaaa!!

'What employable skills do you think you have for the workplace?.....Jawad....'
'I can say the alphabet backwards.'

'Hi, is this Jordan's mum?'
'Yes, what's he done now?!'
'He was really rude in class today, shouting over me, refusing to do work, trying to throw bits of paper into student's ears....'
'Right, I've had enough of this....next time he does this, let me know, and I'll be in that classroom in my most minging tracksuit sitting behind him keeping an eye on him.'
'Thank you for your support, I'll be sure to let you know if there are any further incidents.'

'So class, what adaptations do humans have that make them different from chimpanzees?.....Yes Ella?'
'We don't always eat bananas.'

'What other than food do you need to sustain life?......Josh?'
'Semen'

'Miss your boots are well swag.'
'Thanks Samira. What does swag mean?'
Samira shook her head and looked at me with contemptuous disgust.
(It means cool.)

'Aaaaarrrrrrrhhhhhhhgggggggg, oooooowwwwwwwww'
'Fletch, what did you think was going to happen when you stuck your groin into a rotating fan blade?'

'James, why did you throw that rock at Maz?'
'Well in computer games they always get back up again.'

'Toby, let's hear what your ambition in life is.'
'I want to live in a derelict restaurant.'

'Miss, miss, look at this.'
'That's an ultrasound. Of a foetus.'
'Yeah, I know, I'm going to be a dad.'
'Right. Luke you're 13, have you spoken to anyone about it?'
'Ahhhhahahahahahah!'
'I'm not sure this is so funny.'
'Roasted! It's my mum's, I'm going to have a baby brother!'

'You got that off Wikipedia!'
'I wrote Wikipedia.'

'Lucy can you stay behind a moment please……………………..Are you ok, you are not your usual lively self, what's wrong?'
Sniffle sniffle. 'Something awful has happened!' Sob sob
'Here, have a tissue. Do you want to talk about it?'

Furious nodding, inconsolable sobbing.
'It's ok Lucy, in your own time.'
A few minutes of uncontrollable wailing. 'MY GOLDFISH DIIIIIIIIED!'
Goodbye lunch break.

'Dylan, why are you crying?'
'Sadie stole my favourite sharpie.'

'And that's how we…..'
Sparks. Darkness. Crackle. A yelp from the back of the class.
'Bruce!'
Shell shocked look.
'You are one of the smartest students I've ever taught, you're about to take your physics GCSE, you're predicted an A*.'
'I know.'
'Then why did you stick the scissors into the plug socket?'
'I don't know.'

'MMMIIIIIIIIIIIIIIIIIIIIIIIIIIIIISSSSSSSSSSSSSSSSSSSSSSSSSSSS!'
'Oh my god!' Hit the gas cut off. 'Safiya! Come here!…….Are you ok?'
'Yes miss.'
'What did you do?'
'I put a match in front of the gas tap.'
'Why?'
'To see what would happen.'
'But you know what would happen, you attach the Bunsen burners onto it.'
'I wanted to make sure.'

'Oh, thanks Adrian. Have you given any other teacher a gift?'
'No, just you.'
'Well, in that case, I'm flattered you think I am 'The Worlds Okayest Teacher', as this mug tells me.'

'You're going to have to take your hand away from your mouth, and talk clearly, I can't understand you Mohammed………..Oh I see, how did you manage that?'
'Phwumf, mummmgh, urrggyybbbbbrh.'
'Alright, don't try and talk. Just hold your lips apart and I'm going to slowly uncoil this spring from your braces. Now where's the end…..'

The voice of educators and education students

Balbir Kaur

Balbir Kaur is a lecturer at Brunel University's Department of Education on Initial Teacher Education. She has over 20 years of experience in education and her areas of research interest include STEM in primary education, primary mathematics and mentoring for equality and diversity.

The voice of educators and education students

The yellow brick road

Balbir Kaur

"If we walk far enough", says Dorothy, "we shall sometime come to someplace". The quote from the Wonderful Wizard of Oz, where Dorothy (the lead character) finds herself in a completely different world trying to find her way back home, summarises my thoughts and reflections on a research study that I recently carried out. Stepping into the world of research, in realms of paradigms, with ontological views and epistemological ideas, was a little like being 'cycloned' to Oz. Even though Dorothy is given direction by her munchkin friends, in my case, my tutors, to follow the yellow brick road, she still has to find her way, through trials and tribulations. I am not quite sure where home would be for me, a resident in research where I can locate myself maybe. I am hoping it is a place where I feel some certainty in understanding the concept of 'doing' research; have confidence with the research approaches I plan to take and some assurance that what I am doing is of use and benefit, albeit just for me. The intention of this article is to share my experiences and reflections on the process of 'doing' a small-scale empirical research study. I am hoping you will join me on this short journey along the yellow brick road. I will stop at various points; the purpose and justification for the study, the literature review, the participants or co-researchers and the methodology. You may find

reading this entertaining, or you may find you too have walked along a similar road yourself when planning a research project.

"What have you learned, Dorothy?" (said The Tin Man). Last summer I carried out an action research study on curriculum design for STEM (science, technology, engineering and mathematics) education. The study itself emerged out of curiosity that my colleague and I had around designing learning opportunities in STEM with primary school teachers. The interest was mostly led by the assumption that STEM education in primary settings was relatively naive and undeveloped, as a result, the action research study offered an insight to how STEM education can be initiated as part of a curriculum. We were trying to improve our understanding of STEM and how it could be implemented within a curriculum. I was not alone in the venture.

As each character in the Wizard of Oz had a purpose of walking the yellow brick road, so did the participants in the research. I was curious about the maths in STEM as the resources and plans I saw had minimal reference to that subject matter. I led the study and the direction of the research, I was wearing the ruby red slippers. Scarecrow, my colleague, represented a commercial company that had designed the STEM resource and sought opinion on how the resource was put together. It was him I met first along the yellow brick road. The Lion (headteacher) of a primary school and her year 4 class teacher (Tin-woman) were both interested in developing the idea of STEM education to inform their curriculum. When the four interested parties came together, we were transformed into another world, the world of research, we found our yellow brick road.

As of most journeys taken, there is a purpose, an aim and a destination, and although curiosity and interest are valid reasons for carrying out research, it required a broader scope and ambition.

The voice of educators and education students

Research ought to be considered to be topical, interesting to a wider audience, advance the field and make an important contribution to our understanding and to practice. Therefore it is not just about how the research contributes to knowledge but the impact of that knowledge on others (Cohan et al., 2011). Neither of the participants involved in the study were 'experts' in the field of STEM, we needed some direction, and a path to follow, and along came the good witch - the literature review.

Just as Dorothy began her journey along the yellow brick road, the literature review represented a pathway to assist and arrange my thought processes on the topic. The literature review broadened my understanding and provided context for the study. It identified some of the problems in the field in which the research was being proposed. I was constructing a pool of knowledge by jigsawing new insights and relevant information to create a picture of STEM education. It gave me an idea of what had been written and an appreciation of the critical issues in STEM education and how these related to primary school settings. It was formative and contributed to the actions in the study.

Two key points of reflection emerged when conducting the literature review. Firstly, what I read before I carried out the study was not extensive as it should have been and not as well organised and analysed as it could have been. STEM was relatively a new area of learning for me, and I was not conducting my search on the themes that were required for the research. This demonstrates a lack of planning and understanding of the aims and objectives of the research study. The other factor that hindered my progress with the literature review was time. The time scale to plan and carry out the study was restricted to the confines of the other participants and my workload. Setting out a definite time scale for an extensive literature review at the start of the study is something I will take from this study.

The literature review I carried out after the research was more focused and aligned with my case study because I had a better understanding of the precise issues and topics. As a result, I was able to filter the research to focus on articles that were most relevant to the study. Cohan et al. write that a literature review must be useful to the study and inform the research. The linear approach of a step by step guide to carrying out research often situates a literature review at the beginning of the study. What I found to be of greater value is that although the main body of the literature review needs to be conducted before the research is conducted, the literature review also needs to spiral throughout the process of 'doing' the research. Going back to my literature review during and after the research was particularly valuable as it bridged gaps in my thinking and knowledge that I had not explored at the start of the study.

"Toto did not really care whether he was in Kansas or the Land of Oz..." I considered the various paradigms when planning the study. I found that the qualitative approach based on the interpretivist paradigm was most suited. This approach mirrored my own belief that placed a greater emphasis on social interactions as the basis for knowledge. As the researcher and participant in the study, I was interested in understanding how the other participants understood the phenomenon that was under investigation. The interpretivist approach considers knowledge to be constructed by mutual negotiation and is specific to the situation being investigated (O'Donoghue, 2006). All participants had an invested interest in the research and were seeking to gain new knowledge on STEM education designed specifically for primary school settings.

"Brains are the only things worth having in this world..." The Scarecrow was a colleague and the commercial rep. He had

experience of working in a variety of primary schools. He had since moved to work for a private education commercial company that produced and sold online educational resources to schools. Through this role, he continued to work with schools and was continually engaged with teacher education. His area of expertise was Information Technology (IT). The IT knowledge proved to be very valuable as 'technology' is an area in STEM that came under scrutiny throughout the research. Scarecrow was able to observe the teaching and application of this subject in a more meaningful and more profound manner than the other participants for whom technology was not an area of expertise. It was clear that this research would provide an evaluation of the STEM resource and highlight what worked and what needed changing before it was marketed out nationally and internationally. He had an apparent reason to be part of this journey; he lacked the knowledge.

"True courage is in facing danger when you are afraid..." The Lion was the headteacher; her involvement was minimal in that she was not as involved as the other participants but had an overview of what was happening. The Lion was an experienced practitioner of 20 years and was the headteacher at the school. She was in a phase of making changes within her school in response to the changes that were occurring externally. Ofsted had launched a new school inspection framework, where the concept of the curriculum was high on the agenda. Senior managers were asked to consider the curriculum they were implementing and the impact it had on learners. More so, headteachers had to justify the approach to the curriculum they took. Children were motivated by STEM in her school; however, teachers did not have the resources or the knowledge to implement STEM as part of a curriculum; instead, it was a bolt on to the curriculum. The Lion was brave in taking a STEM approach to the curriculum when very little professional

development and resources for primary teachers were available. Her mission was to persuade and encourage the rest of the staff to join in with her crusade. The insight from this research would offer a model and an idea to base her argument for school development and evidence to share what works and what could be better. She had an apparent reason to be part of this journey; she was developing courage.

"A heart is not judged by how much you love" The Tin-Woman, the year 4 class teacher, was most involved in implementing the resource and reflecting on her lived experiences of how it went. She had an interest in science and therefore offered her insights on science learning and teaching. She expressed her involvement to understand STEM better and to gain some professional development. The Tin-Woman was nominated by the Lion to participate in the research. Her role in the study was to contextualise some of the suggestions. She was recognised to raise the profile of STEM within the school and act as an ambassador of STEM education to support other teachers in the school. She had an apparent reason to be part of this journey; she was developing the passion and enthusiasm for the discipline.

I have positioned myself as Dorothy, the one with the ruby red slippers and the one who started the journey on the yellow brick road accumulating the various participants along the way. I made the initial proposal and led the research, therefore, guided the other participants along the road. The expertise that I brought to the group included knowledge of carrying out a research study. I had over 25 years of experience in education and had some knowledge of curriculum design. My area of expertise is mathematics. The maths knowledge proved to be very valuable as it was one of the four areas in STEM that came under scrutiny throughout the research. I was able to observe the teaching and application of this subject in a more meaningful and profound manner than the other participants for whom mathematics was not an area of expertise. I had an apparent reason to be part of this journey; this study was an opportunity to learn about myself as a researcher.

It can be assumed that this research was motivated by an intellectual interest in STEM to extend the knowledge base of all participants in one way or another. Merriam and Tisdell (2015) refer to interpretivism research as having multiple realities or interpretations of a single event. As a researcher and participant, I was able to gain an understanding of how each participant interpreted their experiences of implementing STEM, putting the researcher in a position as the 'primary instrument for data collection and analysis' (pg. 16). I was able to respond and adapt the research based on the interpretations of the phenomena at various points during the study.

Adhering to a collection of ethical guidelines set by an organisation has increasingly become important in research. Ethics has been defined as a 'matter of principled sensitivity to the rights of others' (Cavan, 1977, p. 810, cited in Cohen et al., 2015). For this study, the Brunel Research Ethics Online (BREO) approval was required before commencing. I found BREO to be a valuable signposting to the study I was about to design as it offered a structure and scaffold to how I was considering planning this research. The participants in the research were willing and voluntarily provided consent.

I want to turn your attention to the choice of instruments used for data collection and my justification for these choices. Merriam and Tidwell (2015 pg. 105) refer to data collection as 'asking, watching and reviewing'. Data that is rich in description and explanation is often labelled as qualitative data. This type of data offers detailed descriptions of people's activities, behaviours and actions (Merriam and Tidwell, 2015 p.105). The use of an interview is considered to be a common form of data collection in qualitative studies. Interviews are regarded to be a social and interpersonal encounter as well as a way of data collection. Kvale (1996, cited in Cohen et al., 2015) categories two types of interviews one, which is the miner, the purpose of which is to extract information and other is the traveller who co-constructs knowledge. As the participants were also co-researchers, and we were co-constructing knowledge and action together, the interview approach taken was that of the traveller. The themes for the interview emerged over the time we carried out this research. The interview allowed these themes to be explored and reflected. I was able to interpret issues in-depth and gain an understanding of the situation. The interviews in this study provided a summary of the whole research. They explored some beliefs that emerged for more detailed scrutiny.

The documents for analysis were the STEM resources provided by Scarecrow, which throughout the research, through reflection and evaluation, developed into a STEM curriculum plan. These were modified and changed over the process of the study. Each change was documented and colour coded to show what had altered and the reasons why. The group discussions often informed the refining of the STEM resource and as a result, was modified to show the changes expressed. These documents painted an interesting picture of how the use of the STEM resource had evolved to reflect the pedagogical and subject knowledge issues that arose. It also provided useful insight into the thought process that emerged and further informed the interview.

"Please, sir, we've done what you told us: we've brought you the broomstick of the Wicked Witch of the West. We melted her". I end my journey on the yellow brick road here having shared with you

my lived experience of planning a research case study. As Dorothy got to the end of her journey, she did not make her way home as intended, the first time. This was a moment of deep reflection for her. As I pause for thought I too feel as if I have not quite got to the end place of being a 'researcher' yet. Did I achieve an outcome from carrying out the research? The participants took something from this study (heart, courage and knowledge) and have taken on board the issues that emerged. Myself, well, I have reinforced my understanding of research and processes involved. I still have the ruby red slippers so getting to that place, where I am well informed with research, is only three clicks away. After all *"There is no place like home."*

The voice of educators and education students

Asgar Halim Rajput

Asgar Halim Rajput works in student support at Brunel University. He is also a part-time lecturer at the Markfield Institute of Higher Education. His interest is in Education and the individual non-academic challenges students face. He is currently writing his doctorate thesis on intersecting issues for Muslim students in English higher education.

The voice of educators and education students

A mature student's experience of higher education

Asgar Halim Rajput

One who leaves school without completing basic secondary school education is considered a 'drop out'. When I left school in my final year just before my exams, the credentials for completing secondary education was known as the General Certificate of Education: Ordinary Level or O level. This was a cycle of eleven years of study to mark the end of Secondary school. O level was introduced in 1951 and replaced in 1987 by the General Certificate of Secondary Education (GCSE) (AQA, 2020). This change was significant for those who wished to leave school at 16 without attempting Advanced level study also known as A Level. My family was in Kenya at the time, a country that got its independence from British colonial rule. Due to its colonial history, Kenya inherited the British curricula (Whitehead, 2006). Fortunately for me, there were no such terms as 'drop out' when I left school. However, for the next twenty-five years, the lack of schooling played on my mind.

The reason for dropping out of school was because the family were British nationals and we decided to leave sunny Africa to go and live in freezing London, which contrary to popular belief, was not paved with gold. Coincidentally, our departure to London would have meant not sitting my O Level exams. So, I did not prepare for my exams. However, due to bureaucracy, our departure was delayed by a few months, until just after my O level exams. As I had not prepared, I did not sit my exams and soon after, we left for London, for good. I spent the next twenty-five years without any qualifications, working menial jobs.

It was in my mid-forties and being bored and tired of menial work, I re-evaluated myself, which I often do, and realised that I had the potential to do much more, particularly in the realm of education. A chance conversation with a colleague turned out he was going on an English language teaching course, Certificate in Teaching English to Speakers of Other Languages (CELTA). My curiosity got the better of me and I inquired about the course. Within a few weeks I had enrolled on the course. It had been twenty-five years since I left school or undertook any studies. It was late March and the three month course was my first step into a long journey of further studies, teaching and training. In September that year, I stepped into a classroom to teach my first ever lesson in English to speakers of other languages. That was over fifteen years ago. Since then, I enrolled on and completed numerous certificate programmes, including a postgraduate certificate and three master's degrees. I lecture two core modules on a master's degree programme in a higher education institution.

I was focussed, determined, motivated and had the drive to continue with my education. I had the bug, as they say. I was also keen to work in an educational environment rather than take any job for survival's sake. This got me searching for jobs in the education sector, primarily college and university. My interest lay in mature young adults rather than school age children. My personal disposition meant that I could engage with mature young adults a lot easier. Thus, my current role, apart from lecturing, is in student support in higher education. This means that my overall experience of education, specifically higher education is that of a student, a professional, and an academic. Next role, vice chancellor? Not quite! I know not to have grandiose notions and simply dismiss them.

Aside from the fact that it had been twenty-five years since I left school without any qualifications, and returned to education in my forties, I had no clue what to expect. I had to learn the stuff of education; new language, academic language, source literature, critical thinking, write abstracts, write assignments, referencing, literature review, methodology, write introductions, write conclusions, new technology, and most importantly learn how to learn, particularly at a much higher level than I had ever experienced. I had to learn about paradigms, philosophical stances, ontology and epistemology and new knowledge. I was a complete novice when it came to study at university.

The first process to study at university was to find a suitable course of study. I was teaching refugees, so when I saw an advertisement for a master's degree course in refugee studies, I decided to inquire and then embark on the programme. Not having a degree did not jeopardise my application as my enrolment was based on life experience, my numerous short courses certificates, and the fact that I was already teaching… refugees in particular. We studied migration patterns, forced migration, immigration and race, spaces of knowledge, and methodology. It was tough going. The learning was challenging. A lot of what was being taught was way above my head. I failed the dissertation at the first submission, but passed on the second. Passing the master's degree was an exhilarating experience. I wanted more. So, I applied to do another master's degree, this time in Equality and Diversity. Having completed the second master's degree, the next step in this educational journey had to be a PhD. Encouraged by my achievements, I applied, got accepted and that was the start of my doctorate journey. And what a journey it has been.

My various experiences in higher education, alerted me to what I now consider to be inadequate support for mature students. At university, all students are treated the same, except for those with disabilities. University enrolment structure is designed for and meant primarily for continuing students; those who have completed A levels. A student who is returning to education after many years, and is not a continuing student, is not supported in the same way as a continuing student. Here, I don't mean support in learning, but support in social issues that a young adult may not face. Mature students are more likely to be married, have a family/children, be in work, and so on. These are huge responsibilities and huge commitments that can be difficult to juggle. All of the above applied to me. I did not have prior knowledge of expectations. There are no instructions of support for a mature student. I did not know who to turn to for emotional support. I did not need a counsellor, or a mental health specialist, but someone who could understand my situation and help guide me through this hectic schedule. I was unable to identify colleagues who had been through a similar situation as I was going through. Everything was in disarray. I asked myself, do universities cater for mature students the same way they do for continuing students? Does enhancing the student experience not apply to mature students? In order to move forward, I had to figure out a strategy that included work, family, and studies; a work – life balance. Like a professor said, plod along one step at a time. However, the plodding along refers to my learning not to my social concerns that impact my studies.

Progress in my studies was immensely slow but with determination, I pushed myself to read and write, as well as ask questions to support my inquiry. I attended additional student skills development programmes, such as speed reading, critical thinking and how to write assignments among others. The additional short courses helped me put my studies into focus, which in turn helped me get organised and progress in my studies. In twenty-five years since leaving school there was no technology. The only technology available then was a calculator and even that was not allowed in the classroom, or students could not afford to buy one. Everything was done manually. Now, I had to familiarise myself with a computer and its programmes; Windows, emails, Moodle, Turnitin, and searches. It was not going to be easy.

Conclusion

Every student needs to be supported during their studies and not just in their learning. Students should be supported in how they can manage their busy lives in order to successfully complete their studies. Universities provide personal tutors, counselling services, mental health experts, disability and chaplaincy among other services to support students. Even students with poor English language skills are supported through the university academic English programme. Students who are not up to par with their studies, can enrol on a pre-sessional course during the summer break. Students can also enrol on study skills programmes available throughout the year. However, as a mature student returning back to education after a long period of time, and as a family man also in work, I could have personally benefitted from learning to manage my life alongside my studies. It would have also been helpful if someone who had a similar experience told his / her story of how they managed their studies. What strategies helped and what did not.

References

AQA (2020) *O-level explanation of results.* Available at: https://www.aqa.org.uk/exams-administration/about-results/certificates/aqa-certificates?a=67789 (Accessed: 28 January 2020).

The voice of educators and education students

Najwa Iggoute

Najwa Iggoute is a doctoral researcher at Brunel University and a lead for psychology and vocational courses curriculum at Fulham Cross Girls' School. Najwa is a psychology graduate, and soon after her bachelor degree, has decided to pursue a master's Organisational Psychology. She then joined the teaching profession in 2008 and has been in the education sector for twelve years. Najwa is an advocate for wellbeing, flexible working and women empowerment, having spent all the teaching career at a girls' school.

Struggles of a mother and teacher: swimming against the tide

Najwa Iggoute

Every day, I used to experience pure guilt - trying to balance my identity as a teacher, as a mother of two boys and as a successful and inspirational woman for all the students I teach. Is that even possible? For the past eight years, since the birth of my first child, I tried with all honesty, I admit that I failed.

Is it my fault? Absolutely not! I blame the system - a hypocritical system where teachers - with a 75% majority of women, are expected to nurture other people's children from every possible angle: academically, emotionally, psychologically, whilst not providing them with an opportunity to care for their own. Nurturing our students is, of course, the right thing to do - after all, we are developing the next generation, and it is indeed vital to support future generations effectively, particularly those students who don't have the right support at home. However, extremely distressing that, as a result, our own children are pushed to the side.

Children of teachers receive secondhand nurture and should be given some medal for putting up with this. A typical teacher gets home in the early hours of the evening, after perhaps a long commute, dragging a heavy load of exercise books in their backpack and feeling drained. The only thing they have left to offer to their children are a few nods and mutters here and there before falling asleep on a sofa whilst trying to gulp a cup of tea and simultaneously speed marking sixty-odd copies of end-of-topic assessments. Forget about reading bedtime stories, bubble baths, healthy conversations about what went on at school, feelings and endless questions. A typical teacher signs their children's school letters after the deadline and attaches an apology note to it, forgets to respond to birthday invitations and occasionally forgets to order their children's lunch despite the email reminders from the school's catering company. What teachers are perhaps great at is buying their children's teachers end of term presents - as they unconsciously and consciously empathise with them - and more accurately - feel sorry for them.

Unfortunately, the education system has been reduced to mere documents and checklists, governed by strict rules and one size fits all policies which obstruct the healthy functioning of young families and hard-working parents. In many schools, simple requests for time off to undertake basic parental duties are frowned upon, such as picking up children from school if childcare arrangements go wrong, attending mothers' day assemblies, caring for them when they are sick... I am lucky to be working at a school with inspirational female leaders who have young families themselves, who understand these daily struggles and who, as a result, have set up a system which allows a good degree of flexibility - but this is, unfortunately, not common practice in other schools. Is this fair? Is this all worth it? Am I happy being a teacher? Am I going to be a teacher for the rest of my life? Most of the time, my answer is 'no'.

Full-time teaching is draining- it is steadily taking away my youth and has turned me grey after two years of joining the profession. It is taking me away from what matters the most in my life, and frankly, is now becoming too prescriptive and boring. Do I want to leave? I wish! There is, however, an unexplained force that keeps pulling me back. Being a teacher is like being on a continuous rollercoaster: it's fun, it pumps up the adrenaline, but too much of it can make you sick.

I am an ambitious thirty-six-year-old woman who has been teaching for the past twelve years. I am now a middle leader but have no interest in senior leadership, not because I am not competent but because that is not the direction I intend to go. What is my next step? What options is this profession providing me at this stage of my career? How do I keep momentum? Well, in 2017, I have decided to take matters in my own hands and take the first step. After all, if you don't ask, you don't get. I decided that the only way to find the right balance, maintain my wellbeing, spend more time with my children and to reignite my brain cells with new challenges, is to request a flexible working pattern. After a hearty discussion with my boss, my request was accepted, with an acknowledgement that I am a long-serving and valuable member of staff, the school would not want to lose. I felt extremely empowered after that conversation. My boss is a hard-working woman who has fought hard to get into her position after devoting all her life to serving the community. She admitted that when her own children were young, she missed many important moments and regretted not being able to do any school runs. At the time, this type of conversation was banned at work. My boss is extremely supportive of parents and is doing her best to make positive changes in support of her staff. In the current situation, teacher retention is a big challenge and providing opportunities for flexible working is a great step to tackle this issue.

Since then, I have enrolled myself on a part-time doctorate of education degree at Brunel University. I am also spending more time with my children, and on my day off, I happily wear leggings and trainers to take my children to school, at regular school hours. I watch their smile as they wave goodbye and enter their classroom. Their teacher now knows who I am and fills me in on progress and occasional friendship issues like she does with other mothers.

Life is still tough for women in 2020. We still have to fight to prove ourselves, jump over hurdles to find the right balance, sprint around tight corners to make things work, and sadly, we don't get a medal at the finish line. In fact, I've stopped caring about medals, credit and recognition. I do what I do to make children happy. Over the years, I taught thousands of students; I still remember their names and they still remember mine. When I bump into them, they rush to hug me, and together we reminisce - and that is the reason why I am still in the profession and will probably always be- as long as flexibility has provided. I have never been happier, more creative, more sufficient and organised at work. Because I feel less guilty, I have more time to recharge my battery, I switch off and, most importantly, my children are much more joyful.

Flexible work is about developing a happier, more engaged and more productive workforce - a workforce equipped with positive mental health, enabling them to nurture, love and successfully teach future generations.

Jin Jiang

Jin Jiang, from Xi'an Polytechnic University, China, is an academic visiting scholar at the Department of Education, who is highly interested in how to introduce technology into teaching and learning. She has been a teacher of English for 16 years. She enjoys the process of teaching and communicating with her students and always believes that her interest is in being the best teacher of students.

The voice of educators and education students

Why do I always want to be a teacher?

Jin Jiang

If you ask me why I want to be a teacher, I'd like to tell you that when I was in high school, I made up my mind to be a teacher under the influence of my maths teacher, Mr. Luo. Mr. Luo is a humorous-strict teacher and it seemed that he knew all the ways to draw every student's attention to his class. Although maths was so tough for us, we enjoyed his class and respected him a lot. He is the teacher and a guide who shows us the world of mathematics; at the same time, he is a friend to us. If anyone can get the top-three scores in any maths test, Mr. Luo would treat him/her the local delicious foods in the restaurant. You can imagine what an honour it was at that time. Whenever he was free, he would visit each student's home in order to know them better. From that very moment, I made the decision to be a teacher. I would like to be a teacher like him who makes friends with students.

What do I think is the most important thing in teaching?

With the fast development of society, students nowadays are quite different from the ones a decade ago. They are more assertive and use the Internet much more frequently to socialise and entertain. They are not satisfied with the current teaching model in China, the teacher-centered teaching model, and expect a more participatory and interactive teaching model.

In my opinion, no matter what age we are in, "INTEREST" is the best teacher for learning. In order to enhance the students' interest in learning, I would like to try new teaching methods to attract students' attention in my class and I want them to be highly involved in activities online and offline.

What have I done in introducing technology into teaching?

I have established four English online learning platforms since 2015, including a Wiki cross-cultural English learning platform, an integrated platform for learning and testing, an online 'English corner' of Xi'an Polytechnic University (XPU), and a CET-4 (College English Test-Band 4) learning website.

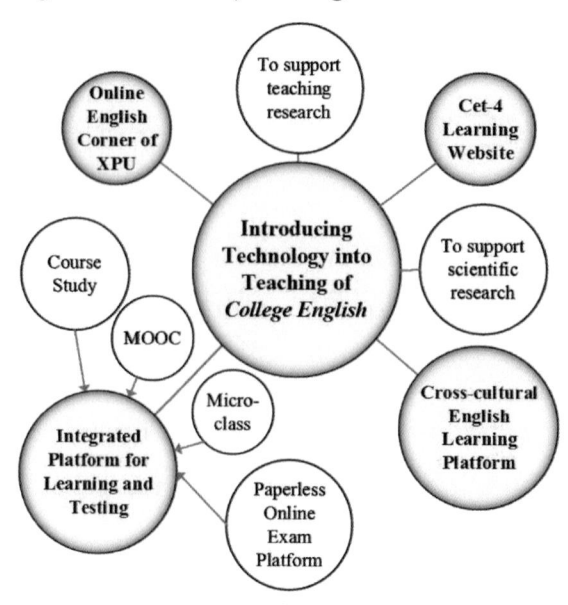

Figure 1: Introducing technology

By introducing technology into education, my team members and I tried our best to help our colleagues change their teaching concepts, carry out new technology-based teaching management, reform examinations and assessments, and provide a new path for student-centered individualised autonomous learning.

One example of what I have done these years: Using Wiki Technology to Construct a Cross-cultural Communication Learning Community

With the help of Wiki technology, a student-centered cross-cultural English learning platform has been established, which breaks the traditional teacher-centered cultural teaching model restricted by classroom and time. Relying on the network platform for cross-cultural communication, students are encouraged to learn cultural themes by way of group cooperation, peer mutual assistance and collaborative communication to arouse their enthusiasm for learning. My project is divided into two parts, the empirical and investigative, as follows:

1. The empirical part of my project will be conducted in the following five phases:
   ① **Preparatory phase** (to analyse the characteristics of online platform learning and to clarify specific teaching tasks, evaluation methods and evaluation indicators etc.)
   ② **Start-up phase** (to clarify the cross-cultural themes and to arrange cultural learning tasks etc.)
   ③ **Collaborative phase** (learners collaborate and communicate through the platform and solve problems together etc.)
   ④ **Teachers' guidance phase** (to offer guidelines and assistance in learning skills, methods, and other relevant questions etc.)
   ⑤ **Teachers' evaluation phase** (to give an overall evaluation, task evaluation, question feedback etc.)

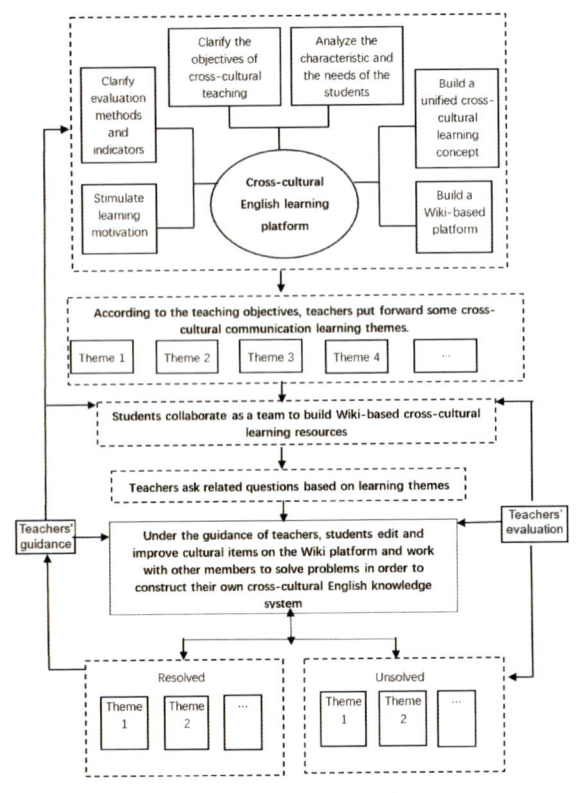

Figure 2: the empirical part of my project

Figure 3: Cross-cultural English learning platform

2. By collecting feedback from learners on the effects of using the platform, we then conducted an investigation from the following three aspects:

① **Social and cultural test**: In order to compare students' mastery of cross-cultural knowledge before and after using the Wiki platform, we organised multiple social and cultural tests for students, and used SPSS 19.0 software for data analysis to draw true and reliable conclusions.

② **Questionnaire**: In order to collect feedback from students in the process of using the platform to learn cross-cultural knowledge, we designed multiple sets of questionnaires. By analysing the feedback, we fine-tuned the structure and functions of the platform to further improve the platform construction.

③ **Empirical research data analysis**: One experimental class (60 students) and one control class (62 students) were selected. The experimental class adopted a cross-cultural teaching model based on the Wiki interactive platform, while the control class followed the traditional English culture teaching model.

At the end of one term, independent sample t-tests were performed on the social and cultural test scores of the two classes. The test scores of the experimental class were significantly higher than those in the control class, and the difference was statistically significant ($t = 4.126$, $P < 0.01$).

What are the issues I look forward to solving in the near future?

From my point of view, the traditional classroom teaching model alone cannot meet the needs of college English learning in the 21st century. The questions are how to carry out blended teaching in a university and how to combine the advantages of traditional learning methods with the advantages of e-learning are urgent problems that need to be solved in front of us.

Finally, I would like to say that I am honored to have the opportunity to visit Brunel University and I want to thank Professor Mike Watts for giving me the chance to introduce my tJiangeaching experiences here.

The voice of educators and education students

Pauline Sithole

Pauline Sithole is currently an ESL/EFL teacher to young learners and adults in London. In addition to this, she has also worked as an EAL and SEN teacher in state and private, primary and secondary schools. She earned a Bachelors degree in Education from London South Bank University, continuing on to receive an MA TESOL from Birkbeck College, University of London and a Postgraduate Certificate in SEN Co-ordination from Leeds Beckett University. At present, she is a PhD student in the Education Department at Brunel University, London.

The voice of educators and education students

A daring adventure

Pauline Sithole

There are several versions of this quote but, despite this, the message by this fascinating yet at times controversial educator is the same, avoiding danger does not necessarily reduce it and life is an adventure to be lived. However, as educators we are sworn to a duty of care and it is required that we safeguard our students to the best of our abilities. By doing so we ensure effective learning takes place and that this and other factors contribute to their holistic, positive development.

> *'Life is either a daring adventure or nothing. Security does not exist in nature, nor do the children of men as a whole experience it. Avoiding danger is no safer in the long run than exposure'.*

As teachers, we employ multiple techniques to engage our students in the classroom and to help facilitate their learning. We are aware pupils have different learning styles and at times, although we may put a lot of energy into a classroom lesson, we secretly know that some students just do better outside of it. Hence, thankfully, the school trip.

According to the online Collins dictionary (2019), a school trip is 'an outing or holiday that a school organises for school children'. Often times the term field trips are also used. Despite this, it is implied that a group of people, in this case students, embark on a learning activity outside of their usual learning environment.

The organising and facilitation of a school trip by the activity or school trip co-ordinator or educator can raise a number of questions and concerns. Issues surrounding the needs of the student population, methods of transportation and determining optimal routes, school, parental and student consent, risks and risk reduction, location and navigation within the external learning environment may have a significant effect on the school trip itself prior to, during and after it.

As astute as Helen Keller's (1940) statement is, this unpredictability within the world should not be seen as a reason to avoid or resign oneself to harmful events. School trips, if planned well, can complement classroom learning wonderfully. They are flexible and can be used with students of various age groups, language abilities and numbers. However, the purpose of this article is to examine how they have been used by this educator in her practice.

It is always daunting for a person to move to a new country especially if it is one where the dominant language is not their own. Students of varying ages with or without a support system will encounter a number of challenges as a result and school trips can at times be used to help students adjust to the environment outside of school and give them a different perspective other than the one they would get from their family, friends or other members of their communities.

There are many legal issues to consider when planning school trips and it is highly recommended to consult not only the school but external agencies when doing so. The Health and Safety Executive

(2011) provides useful information about school trips and as with Keller (1940) also agree that fear of danger or bureaucracy should not prevent them from occurring. 'Well-managed school trips and outdoor activities are great for children. Children won't learn about risk if they're wrapped in cotton wool' (Health and Safety Executive, 2011).

Having decided on the location of the school trip it is often advised by professors on teacher training programmes for educators to visit the location prior to the trip itself. This is exceptionally good advice and it is always also a good idea to keep the school's safeguarding policies and procedures in mind when doing so. Figure 1 is an example of a risk assessment used by the school.

The document requires staff members to examine the risks before control measures are put in place and what level of risk it is. After this, staff are required to evaluate control measures that can be put in place to reduce the risk and after such actions the level at which the risk would have

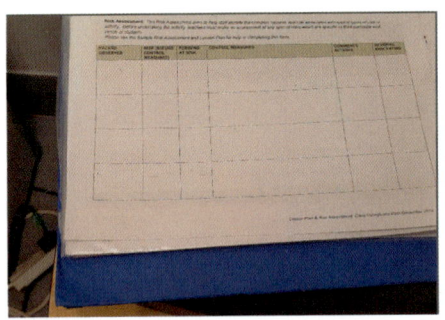

Figure 1: School trip risk assessment

fallen too as a result. As stated in the above quote by Helen Keller (1940), risks in our environments do occur whether anticipated or not but as advised in teacher training and by schools, assessing risks for field trips should be done strategically.

School trips at the worst of times can be logistical nightmares. Obvious reasons for this - aside from it simply being the 'School of Life' - is not practising the journey and anticipating problems. Additionally, failing to inform students and or parents about the nature or purpose of the field trip, activities, expenses and the like. Another reason could be underestimating staff to student ratios and any additional needs students may have and how to manage these. Behrendt and Franklin (2014) stress the importance of enhancing the school trip experience by anticipating and planning activities before, during and after a 'field trip'. Their argument is that by doing so 'students who directly participate during a field experience generate a more positive attitude about the subject'.

It is not only the students' attitudes that may be affected too. An educator who is a survivalist at heart could enjoy a field trip, going into the unknown with their band of young students, packed for any eventuality and ready to tackle Knowledge as and when it surfaces. Bear Grylls would be proud. Having established your strategy of movement the next important activity is determining how to make the most of the location. The most frequent question we are asked in our context when planning a school trip is 'How does this fit into the learning?' EAL and ESL/EFL learners are often encouraged to use the language they have learnt within classrooms. In addition, to this they are advised to use the language in a number of contexts and this learning-through-usage model is upheld within many language schools (Rahnama and Mollaei, 2012). The following are examples for where the school trip has complemented classroom learning. Local art exhibitions and art galleries are an invaluable way to incorporate language, history and culture and language points can be integrated into the experience.

As shown in Figure 2, our school requires the trip to have some linguistic value, in order to consolidate learning. The school trip planner demands that the teacher defend their event as though they were standing in a court of law and pleading their case. At first, this appeared to be an inconvenience, however as time went by it was discovered that London and its venues offered students vast

The voice of educators and education students

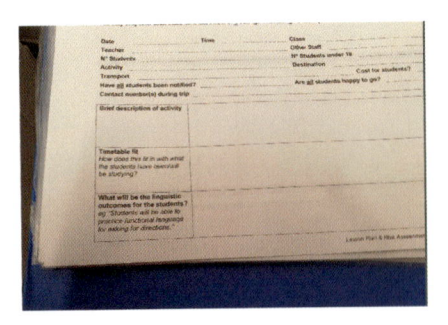

Figure 2: School trip plan

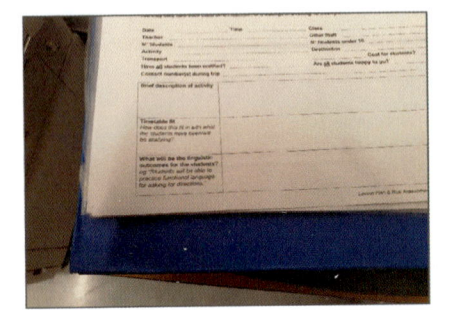

Figure 3: School trip lesson planner

opportunities to use their language skills.

Teaching, it is often said, involves a great deal of paperwork. In spite of this, if one is fortunate enough, planning can begin to refine educators' techniques developing them into a far more effective 'learning and teaching' strategist regardless of their environment. The above planner in Figure 3 has helped in such regards. The trip organiser is required to strategise their activities and materials. For example, it may be observed that particular group dynamics within a classroom may have become static or destructive. Students may have become accustomed to people from within their own grouping or complacent towards finding answers from different sources, for varying reasons. Placing students into temporary groups may force them to discover alternative or detailed answers or consolidate their earlier belief that their group is adequate for their learning needs.

After having provided the rationale for the grouping the teacher may create worksheets incorporating various language points learnt throughout the course. Mastering basic language skills are often abilities people proficient with language take for granted.

A history, art and language class may require students to search for a particular individual in artwork or a piece of artwork within an art gallery. Students in the activity may be required to ask for forms and obtain additional information about a piece. Furthermore, they may be asked to describe the piece, reviewing shapes, colours and objects

Figure 4: Photograph from The National Gallery

or nouns. The lesson may go even further requiring them to use adjectives of personality and age, for example. Students may be asked to speculate about possible familial bonds or not, such as 'this is the father, and this is the son. The father looks happy' (Figure 4). Additionally, students could examine more detailed paintings and revise verbs, describing the actions of the characters.

As mentioned earlier the school trip may help create a more positive attitude towards a subject (Brehendt and Franklin, 2014). A presentation on the piece of work or a short role play interpreting the situation within the piece could be an exciting way to further enhance their interest. Either way, a good school trip is fun, but an exceptional school trip and subject may be remembered positively for years to come.

References

Behrendt, M. and Franklin, T. (2014) 'A review of research on school field trips and their value in education', *International Journal of Environmental & Science Education*, 9, pp. 235-245.

Health and Safety Executive (2011) School trips and outdoor learning activities: tackling the health and an safety myths. Available at: https://www.hse.gov.uk/services/education/school-trips.pdf (Accessed: 13 February 2020).

Keller, H. (1940) *Let us have faith*. Available at: https://quoteinvestigator.com/2014/11/21/adventure/ (Accessed: 13 February 2020).

Mollaei, F. and Rahnama, H. (2012) 'Experiential education contributing to language learning', *International Journal of Humanities and Social Science*, 21(2), pp. 268-278.

X School (2018). *School Trip Lesson Plan and Risk Assessment*. London: X School.

Tawinan Saengkhattiya

Tawinan, who you can also call Fern, is a first-year doctoral researcher in the Education Department who joined Brunel University London in 2019. She grew up in Chiang Rai, Thailand. Her background is in microbiology and she is interested in science education and science communication. She is also passionate about science gifted development and STEM activities for sustainable development. She works as a member of the academic staff of The Institute for the Promotion of Teaching Science and Technology, Ministry of Education, Thailand.

Curiosity - the magic wink in children's eyes: an observation story by me

Tawinan Saengkhattiya

I am quite sure that you have heard the fact that every child is born curious. You might have recognised it in yourself at some point in your lifetime. Some of you are a mother, and you might be familiar with the behaviours of your baby. The baby seeks and looks up to a stranger's face when hearing new voices. Some of you realise that your child always stays up late at night and waits to hear the ending of the mysterious story being told at the bedtime. If you look at the school playground, you might see young explorers digging the sandpit to find anything that is hiding down there. At the same time, young biologists prefer to spend time in the school garden and observe different kinds of spring flowers and colourful butterflies.

It happens spontaneously! Such curiosity lies behind the learning behaviours of homo sapiens - is strongly motivated from the inside and then simultaneously expressed as a biological and physical function. The mechanism behind this behaviour is not yet clear. I will leave explanations for the psychological and biological sciences. What I do know is that curiosity has a relationship with learning. It is an eagerness to know, leads to information-seeking and knowledge exploration. And someone has called it "the hungry mind", which means the desire to pursue knowledge, facts and information.

It has happened to me several times. When I moved to the UK from Thailand, I was so excited - but I was more curious about life here! A bunch of questions had popped up in my head. I seek lots of information about the UK, including how to survive here, how to find food, and how to find a doctor if I was sick. I discovered such information by asking Thai people who already lived here, asking British people who moved to Thailand, searching the Internet and guidebooks. I realised my curiosity is one of the driving forces for learning new things and it is very special. I used to be like that when I was young, and it was very long ago that I walked into my grandma's rice field and looked for species such as crabs and grasshoppers. I recall those times in school when I had such strong impressions of the Biology class - I wanted to know more about novel living organisms. Maybe this was the reason I chose to study microbiology in my undergraduate years.

In my working life, the word 'curiosity' is still attached to me! I have worked to instruct hands-on science activities for the children in different Thai schools. The kids I have met are from schools with very different geographical backgrounds. Some come from the faraway mountain areas where they have to walk for 6 hours to the local centre to join my summer science camps. Some come from the three restricted provinces in the southernmost part of Thailand, where there is danger from ongoing terrorist attacks. To come to join the science camp I organise, soldiers had to take them by the army bus. Some come from different hill tribe groups near the border between Thailand and Laos. Their teacher drove the four-wheel-drive truck from the school to the camp's location. Not all kids I have taught, though, are from disadvantage areas. Some are from Bangkok, the capital city. Some are from areas of high economic growth. At this point, I would like to insist that no matter where they are from - remote areas or central - they undoubtedly have the same thing which I noticed in their eyes. The winks, the clear glassy bright eyes were showing 'curiosity'.

Needless to say, this is why I affirm that curiosity is the key to instruction in science camp activities. In order to lead all my students in reaching the objective of the activities, learning knowledge and the scientific method, being fully engaged with the programme, I need to ignite their curiosity from the very beginning. No need to command, they suddenly turn their body and heads, listen to the guide's instructions to fully participate in the tasks given without showing any signs of boredom. Surprisingly, they start to ask questions.

To catch the kids' curiosity, we tell exciting stories such as new discoveries or relate attractive life stories to 'heat up' the students. An example is when I have introduced "Landing on the planet", which is adapted from a NASA space touchdown activity. In order to land on a planet that has gravity similar to Earth's, students were asked to invent a spacecraft using a paper cup, paper, straws, rubber bands under the constraint to land on the ground safely without

The voice of educators and education students

losing any chocolate balls inside (assumed astronauts). They were enthusiastic after watching the animation about the NASA Curiosity Rover that landed on Mars. The video shows the landing shot that made them go "Wow!!!". When the story was ending, their curiosity sparked their observations by flying paper at different angles, horizontal and vertical. Moreover, I asked them to see objects or living organisms around that fly and land safely. Birds, aeroplanes and frisbees are the most frequent answers. This helped them successfully create wonderful air resistance systems for their non-engine spacecraft. They learned from this activity about gravity and air-resistant forces and engineering design processes.

Occasionally, I skip storytelling but spark the kids by using their senses to play and feel. "An amazing corn-starch" is an activity that needs no complex materials, but only water and corn-starch mixed in a bowl. The white clay-like fluid was ready for them to discover by putting their hands into the mixture to feel its characteristics. Every kid revealed the same answer that this mixture is in a liquid state. Consequently, they were then asked to use their hands to punch the liquid firmly. The fascinating emotion appeared suddenly when they felt as if they had hit a solid surface. The question then arose as to why this happened. After playing around by hand, they had assumed that this fluid could change state when facing different kinds of forces. We call it a non-Newtonian fluid. Another amazing thing I found during this activity was that some of them asked to take the starch back home. Some of them even realized that they have it in their kitchen and it is in recipes to cook a Thai dish called "Lad – Nah", a Thai style noodle in a thick sauce. I am sure that some of them will continue discovering more about the non-Newtonian fluid in the future.

Fun and unbelievable scientific facts are also attractive. An illustration of this is when I ask children if they know of any material that can cry and make a noise. They obviously did not agree with me. So, I let them do the experiment called "why some materials make loud noises". They had to put the materials provided onto some dry ice and investigate which type of materials created a scream. I heard a lot of noise from every group. They switched to wearing gloves and put different kinds of materials in dry ice. They finally found that the metal can make a noise because it can transfer heat. The heat leads to the evaporation of the gas (CO_2) of dry ice. When the gas rises, it turns into pressure between the dry ice and the materials, and that causes a screaming sound. They had so much fun and curiosity at the same time.

From this experience, I can see there is no broad line for curiosity. It occurs with no relationship to the background. A student who has never been on an aeroplane can see a bird fly and observe the wings creating air resistance forces. Indeed, none of them has experience of a spacecraft. They do have the same thing which I found in their eyes, curiosity, that stimulates them to learn. However, their background may affect ways to nurture them in maintaining their curiosity through life.

To sum up, in my view, I am convinced that most kids naturally have curiosity, and it brings benefit to them in whichever state of learning. Remarkably, most of my concern lies in how to nurture them in maintaining a hungry mind. Curiosity can be developed, but, at the same time, it is possible to disappear. Environmental factors such as family and teachers can shape children in having more or less, by allowing them to explore and ask questions. Knowledge should not be just that nominated by teachers, and we need to decrease the 'sit and learn' culture in classrooms. This could enhance and enrich this ability of children and lead them to be highly motivated to learn in their life-long journey. Finally, as an educator, I will reboot my own curiosity and continue finding ways to keep my students curious. I think I have fallen in love with the blink in their eyes.

References

von Stumm, S., Hell, B., and Chamorro-Premuzic, T. (2011) 'The hungry mind: intellectual curiosity is the third pillar of academic performance', *Perspectives on Psychological Science*, 6(6), pp. 574–588.doi: doi.org/10.1177/1745691611421204/.

Engel, S. (2015) *The Hungry Mind : The Origins of Curiosity in Childhood*. Cambridge: Harvard University Press.

Rachel Milburn

I am a first year part-time student, starting my research in January 2020. I studied for my undergraduate degree at the University of Exeter and continued to further my research within my Masters degree in Education through the Open University. Previous roles within education have been 'Assessment Lead' across trust schools and 'Assistant Headteacher.' My current position is working on behalf of the Department of Education as a 'Teacher Trainer Adviser' and it is the realm of teacher training and recruitment that I will explore in more depth within my doctorate.

The voice of educators and education students

A new dawn

Rachel Milburn

Just because one door is open does another door have to close?

Perhaps it was the tedious stop-start of the clutch that made me weary, the M25 had again, made me it's prisoner. The restless slumber the previous night had certainly darkened the shadows that seemed to be a permanent fixture of my dull eyes, sunken upon my over sun kissed face. Oh how I have aged! Did I still recognise the image reflected before me or had I become a grey shadow of more former self, mimicked within the sky above?

The path I had pursued up until this point was certainly not easy, far from it. Yet at that moment, I longed for it, to step back into the rhythm of life I was accustomed to. To walk the hallways as an Assistant Head teacher, to hold my daughter's hand and be mummy, to guide future teachers within my current position. This I knew -this I was comfortable with.

I looked again. The door opened as if inviting me in, welcoming me. I felt the courageous lion within slowly stir and caught a glimpse of the sparkle in my eye, once so full of confidence, stare defiantly back at me.

I reminisced about my journey thus far, dancing in and out of academia from supporting my initial learning as an undergraduate to improving my pedagogy as a professional. A diverse range of opportunities from universities, in-house training and courses galore not to mention the experiences of life. I apprehensively stood there. The ambition had not diminished; it was a character trait. The fire within, grit and determination was what made me me, and it was resurfacing.

Inching closer, grasping for the handle, my mind-set shifted as if the sun's rays were piercing the looming clouds. Hope. Courage. Aspiration.

I was greeted by a smiling face and the words "welcome to Brunel University" echoed in my ears. The journey had not ended, or indeed commenced. I was still on it, just this time it was in pursuit of a PhD and although there were doubts and plenty of insecurities, I had proven myself time and time again and this time will be no exception.

Just because one door is open it does not mean another door has to close.

The voice of educators and education students

Shane De Fonseka

Shane De Fonseka is a third-year doctoral researcher at Brunel University. Having held senior management positions within the UK's private higher education sector for over 12 years, Shane currently works as the Academic Director for London School of Business and Finance. Prior to becoming an academic, Shane managed hotels and international resorts for over a decade. His qualifications include an MBA and a Master of Arts degree in Hospitality Management. Shane is extremely passionate about conservation, recycling, and finding innovative ways to save energy. Shane's leisure time is spent in working on his vegetable allotment, taking photographs and travelling off the beaten path.

Beware the demon in the well

(Ancient) Sri Lankan superstitions, and their modern day explanations

Shane De Fonseka

Growing up in a suburban household on the island of Sri Lanka in the 70s, my childhood was surrounded by many fascinating events, which included a plethora of "don't do it!" or "you should always…" warnings and cautions which were mostly based on superstitious beliefs. Looking back over four decades, I realised that some of these superstitions may actually have some factual significance. This article is an effort to interpret and understand some of the stories I've been told as a child.

Before you clean the well, you should always check whether a demon lives inside it

When attempting to clean old wells or abandoned mines, the elders advised workers to check for demons who may reside in the well. This was done by lowering a lamp or a lantern into the bottom of the well. The resident demon who would find the light unbearable would hastily blow out the lamp, alerting workers of his presence and deterring them from entering the well.

From a scientific perspective, if there was not enough oxygen or if harmful gasses such as methane were present inside a well or a mine, lowering a flame would be a very efficient and safe method of determining whether the air was safe to breathe.

You should always eat everything you have served on to your plate; otherwise, you will lose the weight equivalent to that of a dove

This myth applied to both adults and children alike. The underlying rationale would have been to encourage eating and reduce waste. Unlike nowadays, rice and vegetables were not produced en masse, and farmers had to make a tremendous effort to save their crops from disease and pests. Therefore, any form of wastage was not tolerated.

If you are transporting fried meat, you should always remember to take a metal rod to ward off any evil spirits

In ancient times, people believed in evil spirits called "*Perethayas*" who would roam around (invisible to the human eye) causing mischief and mayhem. These *Perethayas* had an insatiable craving for fried meat, causing them to follow any human who was transporting such delicacies. The elders in my village would always warn people to take a metal rod with them if they were travelling with such food.

This superstition would have made sense prior to mass urbanisation and motorised transport, when people had to travel many miles on foot, through jungles and deserted fields. Wild animals such as foxes, wild dogs or leopards would have definitely picked up the pungent scent of meat (especially fried meat), and attacked any person carrying it. A metal rod would definitely have been useful in such an encounter!

It is bad luck if you turn back, once you set off on a journey

Our elders wouldn't allow us to turn back once we left the house, even if we had forgotten something important. They would tell us it is bad luck and we might meet with an unexpected calamity or accident if we did turn back and walk into the house. To this day, I would always ensure that I had no reason to turn back (such as forgetting my phone or wallet). The underlying cause would have been to ensure that people leave home on time and ensure that they take what is necessary for the day in an organised manner.

When building a house, the front door should not directly align with the kitchen door – it is bad luck

In any house, airflow is very important. If the two doors are aligned, airflow is restricted to the rest of the house as it creates a direct path. Having the two exterior doors misaligned can improve airflow to all parts of the house.

When the "Thala" flower blooms, seven nearby villages will suffer from starvation and bad luck

Thala is the Sinhalese (a language in Sri Lanka) name for Talipot palm (scientific name *Corypha umbraculifera*). The palm tree is considered as the largest inflorescence (a cluster of small flowers on an array of stems) in the world. It is a tree that is featured in the "International Union for Conservation of Nature's Red List of Threatened Species". The tree lives for approximately 60 years before flowering for the first (and only) time with several million small flowers which eventually become fruit. Due to its intense fragrance, bees in the vicinity are attracted to the palm flowers. They do not need to fly long distances for nectar as they get more than enough nectar from the palm. Consequently, the absence of the bees is felt in the surrounding villages when the crops produce a poor harvest due to lack of pollination. The villagers thus see the Thala flower as a sign that their crops will be ruined for a very long time. It is a fact that there were many food shortages in the past when a Thala tree bloomed.

You should always pray to the tree spirits for seven days before cutting a tree

In ancient times, it was widely believed that tree spirits (*Ruk devathawan*) resided in trees which they protected. Cutting down or destroying a tree meant evicting and thereby offending the resident tree spirit. In order to avoid such a disaster (tree spirits were believed to be quite vindictive), one was expected to pray to the tree for seven days before cutting it, begging the tree spirit to leave the tree and find another place to reside.

The rationale would be for the seven-day cooling-off period to allow the villager to evaluate as to whether it is absolutely necessary for the tree to be cut. Also, if the tree were suffering from drought or disease, it would give the tree a reasonable timeframe to recover.

Always wash yourself in turmeric-infused water after returning from a funeral

This was a common practice even two decades ago. The antiseptic properties of turmeric are the reason behind this belief.

Turmeric water would also be used to clean the house of the deceased after the corpse was taken away for burial. These rituals were dutifully followed before embalming became common practice, thereby reducing the chances of "germs" caused by decomposition.

Burials should never take place on Sundays and Tuesdays

It is widely believed that it is "bad luck for the departed" if you either cremate or bury the dead on Sundays or Tuesdays. This belief hails from India (which has a strong cultural influence on Sri Lanka), where it is common practice for pyres to be floated down the Ganges. The Brahmins (scholars) bathe on Sundays and Tuesdays, and they wanted to avoid bumping into a dead body in the river. Although floating dead bodies in rivers is not a common practice in Sri Lanka, all Sri Lankans (regardless of religion) avoid having funerals on Sundays and Tuesdays.

Do not drop nail clippings on the floor; otherwise, the owner of the house will become poor

I was told this many times by my grandmother and my mother alike. Even today, I consciously collect all my nail clippings, ensuring that I don't drop any. In reality, this would have been done to deter children from littering the house with their nail clippings, which would have been very unhygienic, particularly in a large household of 10-12 children.

Fuller for longer

Sri Lankans do a lot of charitable deeds. This includes offering cooked food to crows (who are notorious scavengers). It is believed that you can accumulate a higher level of good karma if you offer crows lamp wicks which are dipped in ghee, with their meal. It is believed that the crows will feel full for a longer time. Lamp wicks are not digestible, and the reason for dipping it in ghee is to add flavour, tricking the crow into thinking it is food. Once the crow swallows the lamp wick, it will stay in the crow's stomach for a longer time than regular food, thus making the crow feel fuller for longer. The repercussions of this practice on the health of the crow population in Sri Lanka is yet to be researched!

References

Johnson, D. (1998) 'Corypha umbraculifera', *The IUCN Red List of Threatened Species.* Available at: https://dx.doi.org/10.2305/IUCN.UK.1998.RLTS.T38494A10118423.en (Accessed 10 January 2020).

Ling Li

I am a Master of Arts student in Education studying at the University of Brunel. I have many years work experience from overseas banking to multinational companies. I ran a company with my partners in international trade. Three years ago, I landed a job as an education training supervisor in a Shanghai education company where my main responsibility was to develop study plans for students through communication and deliberation with them. In addition, I had to ensure all teachers had access to the training system and participated as required. Although my focus was not on teaching, the experience I gained piqued my interest in the real needs of students and teachers in the same vein. The three-year work experience in education enhanced my interest and placed me where I find myself today.

Training centre experiences

Ling Li

My experience in Shanghai, China three years ago where I worked in an education and training center was enlightening. Our training center uses English as the medium of training. The center offers not only English language training but also other subjects (such as mathematics, physics, biology, chemistry, among others). Personally, I worked with students between the age of 12-16 years old.

As it is well known, most students in this age group have not yet developed a clear sense of direction for their future or decided which major they will study in the future and, finally, the kind of work they will love to embark on when they grow up. They need adults to guide and direct their thinking and learning processes. However, unfortunately, parents are only equipped with general ideas hence the need for teachers to step in. For example, if a child shows interest in biology, he may go to medical school in the future, and if music interests a child then he may want to study music in the future.

Mostly, parents know the child's preferences and interests but are unable to direct and guide them to realize these successfully. In this scenario, parents are advised to consult a training center consultant for searching, application and successful enrolment. The teachers at these training centers have professional knowledge, experience and vision to assist in providing specific learning plans according to the requirements of parents and students.

Moreover, it is worth noting that each student who visits the training center for consultations has a different purpose and reasons unique to them. Some students want to improve their spoken language abilities while others aim to improve their general academic performance, and some students ultimately want to apply to good schools in Shanghai or abroad. This is via the training center's networks and good application records (most students apply to British and American secondary schools).

To illustrate this scenario of some student cases, the following structure is a good example: Student A enters the fifth grade of Shanghai Public Primary School because all courses in public schools are taught in Chinese. Although English courses are offered in public schools, there is usually no English environment created to help with real-world practice. Students normally want to improve their English skills and achieve good English grades in a written exam. When Student A visits the training center, we first conduct a simple interview to ascertain his/her ability. For instance:

> *Q: Why come to the center to study?*
> *A: I am not sure, but I know my English grades are not good. At the same time, my parents hope that I can learn English well because they plan to send me to a university abroad.*
> *Q: Do you like learning English? Do you know what it means to learn English?*
> *A: I don't like it very much, but I know if I learn English well, I will have the opportunity to study abroad.*

The voice of educators and education students

> *Q: What part of English do you want to enhance, listen, speak, read or write?*
>
> *A: I want to improve these parts, but at present I think it is mainly to improve my oral English skills, because there is almost no chance to speak English at school.*

We discuss Student A's requirements and arrange a three-week introductory speaking course. After three weeks, professional teachers will assess the spoken English level. After passing the assessment, follow-up listening, speaking, reading, and writing training sessions will be conducted. First, students must have a certain level of English proficiency, and no student will immediately undergo professional training. We must lay a good foundation, do a good job of students' ideological adjustment work, increase their interest in learning and achieving good results.

Student B was enrolled in the fifth grade of Shanghai Bilingual (Chinese and English) Private Primary School. Both Chinese and English are important in bilingual schools. Some courses are taught by Chinese teachers, and some courses are taught by foreign teachers (mainly native English speakers). Chinese teachers teach Chinese, mathematics, English, etc. Foreign teachers teach English reading, science (physics, biology, chemistry), art, music, sports, etc. All extracurricular activities are organized by Chinese and foreign teachers. Before enrolment for Student B, we first conduct an interview.

> *Q: What is the purpose of studying at the training center?*
>
> *A: I am about to graduate from elementary school and apply for secondary school. I want to be admitted to an international school in Shanghai.*
>
> *Q: Do you like English subjects? Why?*

A: *I like learning English. There are foreign teachers in our school. I usually communicate with foreign teachers in English. I find it very interesting.*

Q: *In bilingual schools, students' English should be good. So, what part of English do you want to enhance, speaking, listening, reading and writing?*

A: *I want to strengthen my speaking skills. At school we still focus on Chinese communication. We can only speak English in foreign teacher courses. I also want to improve my writing skills in class. I want to be able to write an English story. It would be very interesting.*

The center may arrange a one-month speaking and writing course based on Student B's ideas and responses. After a month-long evaluation, we arrange a systematic English course according to the requirements of international schools. Six months later, he will successfully receive an offer letter from an international middle school in Shanghai. International schools in Shanghai value students' English proficiency because all courses in international schools are taught in English. If the student does not have a good foundation in English, the class will be completely incomprehensible. Courses in the training center are directly taught using textbooks and test papers from international schools.

Student C is attending an international school in Shanghai. All courses are taught in English. The school offers international courses: IGCSE and IB courses. Tthe first and second grades of middle school offer basic courses such as English, mathematics, science (physics, biology, chemistry), art, music, sports, etc. However, Chinese language, Chinese culture and history courses are taught by a Chinese teacher. There are many extracurricular activities in the school. The school schedule is based on the English school's schedule. Similarly, Student C will be interviewed before the training.

> *Q: What is the purpose of studying at the training center?*
> *A: I am studying in an international school and I want to study in the UK within two years.*
> *Q: Why is there such a plan?*
> *A: I want to be admitted to a good secondary school in the UK.*
> *Q: You are currently studying at an international school. Your English ability should be good enough. So, what subjects do you want to study besides English?*
> *A: The school has studies in a good English communication environment. I mainly want to improve my English reading and writing skills. Since the school's natural science courses are taught in English, I also want to study English courses in natural sciences. I like biology class and hope to have the opportunity to study and become a doctor in medical school.*

According to the requirements of Student C, the center arranges a three-month English and science course. Upon completion of the assessment, the training center will arrange courses in accordance with the requirements of the British Secondary School Admission Application Exam. Because applying for a foreign secondary school is not the same as simply improving English, a professional trainer is needed to develop a study plan and arrange courses. One year later, Student C will be successfully admitted to a British private high school, which is one of the top 100 in the UK. Trainers need to fully understand the curriculum content and admission requirements of British schools and develop learning plans based on the actual situation of students.

Through the cases and experiences shared above about three

students, we find that because they come from different schools, they have different learning environments and learning goals. Therefore, their training courses and methods are arranged differently and separately to meet their unique requirements. What needs to be explained here is that the main goals of the training is to help students better achieve their learning goals and future interests. Students also learn to communicate with parents and teachers while trainers listen to their ideas and interests to find the best way possible to support them.

Developing different training programmes through communication processes to help them achieve their learning goals was my main responsibility in which I excelled, as I always listened to students'concerns and acted on them. Students willingly and actively cooperated with the learning plans in order to complete the learning tasks efficiently and successfully in the end.

The voice of educators and education students

Yu Wu

MA Education student in Brunel University. Eight years training experience. Volunteer team member of France Consulate-General Shanghai. Participated in the planning and holding of various social activities related to education. Interested in educational psychology and leadership and management of education.

The voice of educators and education students

Some personal insights in my teaching experience: what do children think of their parents?

Yu Wu

Eight years ago, when I was in year two of my university course, I chose to work as a part-time junior English teacher in my spare time at a local children's Cultural Palace. This was known as an extracurricular center with a passion for education and a love for children. I am pleased with this extracurricular activity, not only because I could help more children, but I also helped parents who were busy with work that they had not much time for their children. During this time of being a teacher, some parents who recognised my professional work asked if I could be their children's personal tutor, helping with the homework assigned by their teachers at school. I was asked to teach them the 'weak spots' in subjects that had been exposed during examinations. During this busy period of time, on the one hand, I must also complete my undergraduate studies. On the other hand, I was busy with my work as a teacher in the Cultural Palace and a personal tutor for a number of children which I met at the Cultual Palace. Hard but happy. I like the sense of fulfilment and the feeling of being needed.

The voice of educators and education students

During one tutoring session, a ten-year-old boy was criticised by his father for failing his English test. The father looked at his son's low score and blamed him non-stop for not studying hard enough. The boy burst into tears, saying that "You can't blame me for these! You don't know any of these! How many points can you get?" His father was silent for a short while and then walked away. I asked the boy to calm down and then mentioned to him that it was impolite to talk to his father like that. And this made him sad. Just like we ourselves don't want to be hurt; likewise, we should not hurt others. As the old saying goes by Confucius "do not impose on others what you yourself do not desire". With tears in his eyes, he repeatedly said to me, "My father's English is very poor. He can barely understand English. He can do nothing to help me. Do you know why my classmate can get better scores this time? Both of his parents graduated from famous universities. They can help him with this subject." While he was saying this, he could not bear his excitement, as if he had been greatly misunderstood.

This seems to be a very common unpleasantness between parents and children in their daily lives. Maybe it can easily slip from parents' memory, and then the relationship with their children will soon be as good as before. But I know there's something wrong with the mutual perceptions of what the father and son think of each other. For instance, when learning English, the boy normally lacked self-confidence, felt inferior due to his parents' weakness in English, and he tended to find excuses for not learning English well. After class, I talked about this issue with his parents. His father commented, I really can't speak English. I can only ask somebody for help." As a matter of fact, this father is very successful in his professional life. He is the backbone of the unit in his industry. I have seen plenty of his honor certificates and trophies. Also, he is a very modest person. But in his generation, most people's thoughts are still very conservative and overly modest. People often say that they are not good, even when others give praise, they will say "no, I am not good enough" instead of cheerfully accepting the compliment and saying 'thank you'.

After checking the mistakes on his test paper, I found the poor score was due to his carelessness and misspelling. It's not a problems that can be solved if his father has a good level of English proficiency. So I asked the boy: if your father's English was very good, could you avoid these mistakes? The answer was no. I then asked him another question about what kind of person he thought his father was. He replied, he was very strict and he felt a lot of stress, even for some subjects his father could not understand. The father would always say to him how well other children did. But he was also self-critical in that he did not graduate from a famous school and could not speak English.

This child's story reminds me of another story caused by the sense of inferiority from parents. There was another girl aged 12 years old who also complained about her mother's educational level. She could not help with her studies when she met difficulties. Similarly, her mother is a perfect housewife covering the job of arranging food, clothing, housing goods, and transportation for six family members and helping her husband manage their company's financial affairs. Everything in the house was in good order. This mother, like the father above, rarely expressed herself and was extremely shy. She never said how much she had done for his family. The child did not know how hard it would be to manage the housework as well as deal with the company business. So she did not understand and appreciate her mother.

From these examples, we can see that without enough communication between parents and children and a full understanding of each other's strengths and shortcomings, it will cause adolescent children to have a sense of inferiority. Besides, for parents who like to compare their children to other children, it will undoubtfully bring more pressure to the children. The best solution is that parents should actively communicate with their children, making the relationship more harmonious. They should trust their children and build their self-confidence. Moreover, they should also see the strengths of each child and do not compare to other children. In this way, children will be much more confident in himself/herself as well as his/her parents.

The voice of educators and education students

Anita Sediqi

I study Education here at Brunel.
I grew up in the Netherlands and I am studying in London.
I hope that you enjoy reading my writing.
"Take any oppurtunity that life throws at you".

The voice of educators and education students

My journey of life

Anita Sediqi

I didn't know where life would take me after I decided to experience living in a different country. I lived in the Netherlands for 12 years. These 12 years were the best years of my life. When my parents fled Afghanistan due to the war, I grew up in the Netherlands. The Dutch language is a very sweet language just like the Dutch people. I grew up in a bright, energetic and active environment. I remember my childhood as if it was yesterday. I feel fortunate as my parents gave me a happy childhood whilst adapting to living in a totally different country with a weird language. My childhood was mostly spent going to school, cycling in my neighbourhood and playing with the children that lived in my area. I was the happiest child. "What else could I ask for?" From a young age, I was able to speak two languages. My first language is Dari and my second language is Dutch. I learnt Dutch when I started nursery in the Netherlands. I speak both Dari and Dutch fluently. When I was 12, we made the decision to move to London. I was very excited as this meant a new adventure of a new chapter in my life. We then moved to London.

Once we started our new life in London. I was faced with a couple of challenges. I missed all of my friends that were back home. In Dutch schools, they teach children basic English. Thus, I knew very little English. The biggest challenge for me was to make new friends and also learn English at the same time. In the UK, I started school in year 8. It was hard as I was in a new environment. I didn't know much English and at the same time, I tried to learn at school. I believe that If I didn't experience this, I would have been a totally different person today.

So far, I have lived in London for eight years. I love London but the Netherlands is home. Often, I do visit the Netherlands. Now I go to university and I am studying Education Studies at Brunel University London. I love my degree as I like teaching children and making a difference in their life. I now speak three languages, and sometimes I do mix these up when I am speaking. My advice would be to take chances in life, as these chances equip you to build a positive future for yourself. You may never look back. I am so grateful for my family and fiancé. My parents have worked so hard to give my siblings and me a loving childhood and a good education, despite having their own struggles. My dear uncles have always guided me in life. Last but not least, my loving fiancé who would always push me when I felt unmotivated. If my dear family and fiancé wasn't in my life, I wouldn't be successful today.

Zahrah Mahmood

I am a highly hardworking, motivated and enthusiastic final year student at Brunel University. Currently, I am completing a BA Honours Degree in Education. My years spent at Brunel has allowed me to strengthen my skills such as organisation, reliability and determination.

It's (not) fine

Zahrah Mahmood

Mental Health - a word that scares some
People who want to help say "come, come"
You're stuck in this never-ending life
Contemplating whether to pick up the knife

Every day seems like a drag
When you get up and pack your bag
Your eyes struggling to open, with hair all over the place
People don't even notice when looking at your face

In the morning, you just about make it in
The only seat left is next to the bin
Your lecturer looks at you like "Why are you late?"
The eyes roll back, straight over to your mate

2.5 hours later, you're thinking "When will this end?"
Hoping some food will get you back on the mend
She speaks about the assignment before you go
"Please let me go before I blow"

Running out of the library and avoiding your friend's call
Whilst you're doing so, your tears begin to fall

She finally catches up to you and asks you, "What's wrong?"
You difficultly play along and tell her, "The day's been long"

The act goes so well, but she knows you've lied
Last week she was feeling the same, I think you're tied
Then you make your way to the bus stop in the rain
Hoping the coldness will eternally numb the pain

After a long journey, the bus finally stops
As you walk home, your stomach begins to drop
Beware of the anxious thoughts, "Are they true?"
The way they speak to you is a big enough clue

They don't understand but do I care?
As soon as you get home, they give a glare
You roll your eyes, "What is it this time?"
Their words sting you as sharp as a lime

You take it on the chin and go into your room
Switch off the lights and accept it as your doom
You've had a long day and just want to cry
Maybe you could, if your family didn't pry

Old mistakes hold you down
People rarely see you with a frown
In your head, you deserve a crown
Do they know their words make you drown?

They ask you if you love them, and you do
But on some days, it's normal to feel a little blue
Struggling with deep issues, but no tears fall
Always being told to stay strong and stand tall

Going out to stand on the lawn
You hope to rise at the crack of dawn
Maybe this will be your life
Still contemplating whether to pick up the knife

Sleeping at night is too hard now
Memories replay, "What a fat cow!"
Heartbreaking every single night
Those dreams and wishes don't seem too bright

The night is the worst, your emotions are high
Being asked how you are, but all you can do is lie
You're struggling but how do you say it?
The sound of your soul breaking, bit by bit

Last few years, it's been hard and it's easy to tell
You don't even flinch at the ring of a bell
Family deaths tore you apart
Maybe this is it for the state of your heart

I know this has made you think
The colour of your cheeks now turning pink
Although it seems bad right now, it will get better
No-one should have to read your suicide letter

There are people in your life who actually care
Yes! I mean that, it's not so rare
Speak to them and let go of all your fears
They will reassure you and wipe your tears

So, breathe in and out, take it one day at a time,
Every good day you have, get a jar and put in a dime

Bhavisha Soma

Bhavisha Soma (left) and Michelle Anderson (right)

I have been a full-time teacher for almost ten years in four different English primary schools and have also enjoyed being part of school leadership. I feel lucky to have worked at each of these schools because I learnt from all of them and continue to do so. I am in the fourth year of my doctoral studies, exploring the impact of primary school assessment through the stories of children, parents and teachers. I value all the educational experiences I have had so far, both as a teacher and a learner. However, as with everything in life, I do believe there is room for improvement.

The voice of educators and education students

What a world it could be!

Bhavisha Soma

A poem by a dyspraxia / dyslexic person

Inconsolable pain flowing through every organism within me
Crushing waves of grief splintering my soul
Piercing my heart
Suffocating every part of my whole self
Breath no more
Gone
Gone
Gone

How many layers of grief will torment me
How many more moments will crush me
How many times will I shatter
How will I recover
Breath no more
Gone
Gone
Gone

Written in January 2019 and reproduced here with the permission of the author, Michelle Anderson.

To stay true to the words and experiences of the author, I have refrained from using my teacher mindset to 'improve' this poem before sharing it with you. I have not tweaked it to suit my taste. Nor have I tried to 'correct' the technical elements, for example, by adding in question marks for the questions. This is something that I would be required to do in my role as a primary school teacher.

The voice of educators and education students

I believe that to change this particular poem would not do justice to the intentions of the writer. Perhaps it might also undermine the powerful expression of grief felt by the author at the time of writing.

Upon reading this poem, over a year ago, what first struck me was the title. It jumped out to me that the author defined herself first and foremost as being somebody with dyspraxia and dyslexia. Knowing her well, I understand that she sees these conditions as having been a barrier in her childhood and as an ongoing challenge in her adulthood. Her memories of school are not positive owing to the fact that she was made to feel like an 'academic failure' (*her words, not mine*). She was never encouraged or supported by the school system; she was simply written off like a naughty child, unwilling to learn what was being taught. She says that being skilful at sport was the only thing that saved her from a downwards spiral. It was her chance to express herself freely and the area in which she excelled the most, at the time.

Sadly I have seen and heard these types of stories repeated time and time again through my role as a primary school teacher. Children are made to feel as though they are failures if they do not attain the 'right' marks, grades or targets set for them in assessments of Reading, Writing and Maths. Similarly, class teachers are made to feel they have failed if they do not ensure children are working at or above their age-related expectations (as defined by The National Curriculum in England, Depertment for Education, 2014). In reality, much of this comes down to tick-box exercises. For example, a tick is awarded for using a question mark to punctuate a written question; no tick is given for not using a question mark. I am yet to come across a box for creativity and flair in a child's writing.

Some of the schools I have worked at have striven to offer

opportunities for children to be successful in more ways than just a tick in a box. In my view, most of the negative pressures that do stem from assessment originate from the constantly moving targets set by the government. These are the same targets that result in schools competing nationally and internationally in league tables. They are also the same targets that lead to schools having little choice but to impose on children the relentless testing of Reading, Writing and Maths. This is often at the expense of learning in other areas, such as the Arts. In my opinion, it is a broken system that only benefits the few, to the detriment of the many.

The situation described above, along with the poem by Michelle Anderson, have inspired my poem below. It is written through the eyes of an imaginary child who dreams of becoming the illustrator of a picture book. I do not claim to speak for every child, or indeed any child. However, in my experience as a teacher and leader, I have seen and heard many a child write and talk about similar experiences to those described above and below. One child even wrote an entire fiction story where their homework (preparation for tests) was the evil character to be defeated by good. Michelle Anderson was one such child; she once aspired to become an author.

A child's picture book (without pictures)

What a world it would be!   What a world it would be!
(If this was my reality)   (If I was set free)
An illustrator would be my calling   Success would be mine
(If I was not falling)   (If I was given the time)
A picture book would be my creation   I would sign off with my name
A representation of my elation   I could play the fame game

The voice of educators and education students

What a world it would be!
(If I could be me)
My beloved creation, take a look
(There are no pictures in this book)
I am not allowed to draw
What through *my* two eyes I saw

I am only allowed to draw
The style of those who came before
We study works by artists past
For *my* artwork, I am not asked
And so this picture book is without
My own pictures that cry out

The pictures showing my story
My mind in all its glory
The pictures I am made to hide
Of what I see and feel inside
Page 1, the school week has begun
I wish for a week filled with fun

Page 2, I drag my heels to school
Page 3, I am made the silly fool
Page 4, it begins to get absurd
The numbers, the letters and the words
To me, they don't make any sense
So I put up my guard, my fence

Page 5, I am so very alone
I feel I am standing on my own
For me again, no plain sailing
Once more, I am simply failing
Page 6 makes matters even worse
The next lesson feels like a curse

Double maths in a different room
Bottom set for us buffoons
Page 7, I try not to lose face
Page 8, I dream of art and space
Page 9, now I am back in class
Page 10, back to this awful farce

Fail every test, never the best
Not ever meeting my targets
And so now I have become
The ever so (never so) naughty one
That's what you've done to me
Not letting me be

One last chance, one last look
At my very own picture book
In my wildest dreams,
In my deepest fantasies,
If *my story* was for all to see
What an amazing world it would be!

It is my hope that one day, children will be able to express themselves more freely and positively, without the constant pressures of assessment weighing down on them. I am proud and delighted to say that Michelle grew up to feel happy and fulfilled in many ways. However, not all children have recovered from their negative experiences of learning at school. There are moments when Michelle still feels that she failed school (or that the school system failed her) and that she is still picking up the pieces. In school, her skills were not encouraged and her strengths were not recognised or celebrated. If children's individual creativity and expression were truly valued as a measure of success at school, what a world it really could be!

Joseph Hanley

Joe Hanley is a lecturer in Social Work, with practice experience in adult social work teams. He is currently undertaking a Doctorate in Education at Brunel University London. Joe has a research interest and has written in the areas of social work education and social policy. He also has research interests and undertakes work in the areas of professional development and disaster social work.

The voice of educators and education students

The negative impact of student evaluations on higher education research

Joseph Hanley

Introduction

Recruiting participants for my research was supposed to be straightforward. Sure, I need to worry about consent and confidentiality more than usual, and there is a strong likelihood of researcher imposed bias, but at least I have ready access to participants, something that is not usually the case in research. I see my students all the time, they know me, and I know them. At my fingertips I have their email addresses, telephone numbers, even their whereabouts for large parts of the day. It doesn't seem overly naïve to think that I should have had no problem recruiting student research participants. This has not been my experience. In fact, engaging students has proven to be the most difficult aspect of undertaking research in my Higher Education Institute (HEI). This short reflection will consider a reason why this may be the case, and ironically it will be suggested that it may be our very obsession with measuring every aspect of student university experience that is creating a barrier to engaging students in research that may actually measure that same experience.

Let me take a step back. I am a social work lecturer in a London HEI, and I am simultaneously undertaking a Doctorate in Education (EdD) at the same HEI. Through both working and studying at the HEI, I have undertaken several research studies and projects that involved gathering data from students, both within my department and outside. Without going into detail on the nature of the research studies that were undertaken, suffice to say that I experienced substantial difficulty in getting students to engage. Response rates were 50% or below for all surveys I attempted, which has led me to question their legitimacy. At minimum this suggests that any findings I develop should probably be taken with a fairly large bowl of salt. Indeed it has been recommended elsewhere that all surveys that receive a response rate of below 60% should be disregarded entirely (Fincham, 2008). I have had even less success when attempting to organise focus groups and face-to-face interviews, including having to abandon these endeavours on two separate occasions.

Lazy Students or Inexperienced Researcher?

The knee jerk reaction is likely to be to blame students as being lazy, disinterested, selfish or disengaged. Indeed that would be in line with the way that policy makers in the UK have consistently characterised social work students in recent years, with those from all sides of the political spectrum publically lamenting the lack of quality of students, the need to recruit more intellectually minded individuals into social work and the general failure of university programmes to prepare students. However, this description is in stark contrast to my experience of students, where I have seen students consistently go above and beyond, in both university and placement based work. Indeed, students on social work programmes in England must undertake an extremely difficult and intensive courses, involving two placements of 70 and 100 days alongside their academic work. Furthermore, all our students undertake a dissertation that is based on primary research, and the consistently high quality of these also contradicts any conceptualisation of students as disinterested in research. The premium that social work programmes place on life experience in the application process also means that many students have families, caring responsibilities and work part time jobs alongside their qualification, and the fact that they are able to still achieve success shows that far from being disengaged or lazy, these students are highly committed to pursuing a job in social work, and improving the lives of those they will come into contact with on a daily basis.

The other obvious area of blame would be to look introspectively at myself. As a doctoral student and an early career researcher I do plenty of this already, second guessing every decision and action I take, in particular when things do not go in the idealised way I have laid out in my head. I am acutely aware of how little I know about undertaking research, and this includes the area of gaining access and encouraging participation. However, these early experiences have meant that I now focus more *and more* time and attention to maximising participation. Steps I have taken include limiting the surveys to 5 minutes, taking steps to not gather any data that could possibly identify a student, organizing focus groups and interviews at weekends and evenings, and providing surveys in multiple formats. While these have potentially increased participation in the studies I have undertaken, response rates and engagement remain a struggle.

I am further encouraged not to place full blame on myself by the fact that I am not the only person who has had difficulty engaging HEI students in research. My experiences mirror those of colleagues I have talked to, both within my HEI and externally. Indeed, Nulty

(2008) found that student response rates to surveys averaged 33%, far below the 60% recommendation that was suggested above. Nulty (2008) found that higher response rates were typically only achieved when students were provided with substantial incentives. This again suggests a level of disengagement from students. However, it is important to acknowledge that not all disengagement is passive in nature, and equating student disengagement in this area to laziness or disinterest would be a vast oversimplification. There is likely something more systemic at play here.

Student Evaluations of Teaching

Students in HEIs are consistently asked for their feedback on their course and institution, most frequently through student evaluations of teaching (SET), which generally take place internal to the university, or through national survey data, most notably the National Student Survey (NSS). These evaluations have a very real and significant impact on universities and the people who work within them. Internal evaluations are used to inform recruitment and promotion, changes to curricula and the distribution of funds. The NSS can have an even more significant impact, informing league table, and now feeding into the Teaching Excellence Framework (TEF), a national measurement of quality teaching that will be the basis for the amount an institution is able to charge for fees. This obviously creates substantial motivation for HEIs and their staff within them to get students to complete the evaluations, a difficult task in light of the points made above around student engagement. Students are therefore chased frequently to fill out these evaluations, both electronically and face-to-face, and considering the evaluations are required several times a year, over multiple years of study, it would not be surprising that students feel over evaluated (Nulty, 2008). As an example, students on a two year postgraduate course at my current HEI are asked to complete course evaluations no less than seven time. Then when one of their lecturers comes along and asks students to partake in research that (at least I believe) will have an actual impact on teaching quality, it is not surprising that it gets lost in the ocean of evaluations and surveys that are sent to students.

This could all be fine if there was any actual validity or legitimacy to these student evaluation tools. This is categorically not the case. Research has shown that student ratings of teaching quality are not related to student learning in those same contexts (Uttl et al., 2017). More problematic, however, these evaluations have been shown to be discriminatory in nature, with female and minority ethnic educators receiving consistently lower ratings, and even abuse in the qualitative comment sections (Mitchell and Martin, 2018). This over-evaluation of students is also concerning as it shapes students as consumers, rather than learners, making their satisfaction the central imperative of HEIs. Paradoxically, this has not improved the student experience in HEIs, and only 38% of students believe that their degree is good value for money (Trendence UK, 2018). Student disengagement, therefore, could be considered a rational response, or even protest, against the damaging impact of the marketization of their education.

Conclusion

I have suggested here that we are potentially generating untrustworthy, unethical and damaging data about students at the expense of rigorous, valuable and (potentially) beneficial research. This could be a serious problem as we move forward into uncertain times in higher education, as the data that we value will ultimately shape how we perceive success and failure, and ultimately reform. Therefore, I propose that student disengagement from standardised evaluations should be perceived as an active expression of student discord. Students should be encouraged to make informed choices about the evaluations they take part in, and we should not pretend there is value where there is none.

References

Fincham, J. (2008) 'Response rates and responsiveness for surveys, standards and the journal', *American Journal of Pharmaceutical Education,* 72(2), pp. 43-45.

Mitchell, K. and Martin, J. (2018) 'Gender bias in student evaluations', *Political Science and Society,* 51(3), pp. 648-652.

Nulty, D. (2008) 'The adequacy of response rates to online and paper surveys: what can be done?', *Assessment and Evaluation in Higher Education,* 33(3), pp. 301-314.

Trendence UK (2018) *Value for Money: The Student Perspective.* Bristol: Office for Students.

Uttl, B., White, C. and Gonzalez, D. (2017) 'Meta-analysis of faculty's teaching effectiveness: student evaluation of teaching ratings and student learning are not related', *Studies in Educational Evaluation,* 54, pp. 22-42.

Rich Barnard

Rich has four grown-up children. One identical twin and his elder sister pursued STEM-based education, while the other male twin and younger sister did not. Inspired by the ongoing nature-nurture debate, his personal focus is understanding his children's choices. While Rich's research interest, 'Attitudes towards Science', stems from teaching primary science.

The voice of educators and education students

QTS professional skills tests: to pass, or too passé

Rich Barnard

Abstract

When I started Initial Teacher Education (ITE) on a Primary PGCE course back in 2009, my cohorts were told during an induction session about the requirement to pass statutory Professional Skills Tests (PSTs) before Qualified Teacher Status (QTS) could be achieved.

This contribution is in response to Ineson's (2018) article on PSTs, where she writes specifically about the numeracy test. Here I detail my own attempts at these tests in 2009 and contrast this to the pre-BEd experience of 'David' in 2016. But instead the focus of this article is on the Literacy PST.

Introduction

PSTs are three tests, which had come into effect in 2000, in core subjects Numeracy, Literacy and ICT (Information Communication & Technology). Science, the fourth core Primary subject at that time, simply has the requirement (since 1979) for at least one GCSE in science (UCAS, 2019). At that time, these PSTs were free and attempts limitless. The national press was, however, not impressed, ['*Teachers unable to do simple tests*", Daily Mail (2005)], even though the pass rates then were, after a first re-sit, 96% for Numeracy and 97% for Literacy.

In April 2012, the Department for Education decided to '*remove the ICT skills test, which is no longer needed... (and)... to limit candidates to two re-sits*' for Numeracy and Literacy (DfE, 2011, p.5). '*Pre-entry literacy and numeracy skills tests* (were) *launched... from September 2012*' (DfE, 2011, p.15), with raised pass marks, and these tests then revised for trainees starting in September 2014. A 'dip' in pass rates post 2011-12 that then resulted for Literacy are illustrated in Fig 1. below, compared alongside those of Numeracy from the Daily Mail (2005, 20th August), DfE (2019).

Fig 1. All trainees pass at first attempt ('On Entry' for 2012-13 onwards)

Ineson (2019, p.17) notes that from February 2018 applicants '*would once again have an unlimited number of attempts*', the two year lock-out period was removed while the first three attempts would now be free.

Anxiety and Speed

The anxiety trainees felt towards the numeracy test, Ineson (2019, p.16-20) suggests, is related to the speed requirement of its timed questions in both mental arithmetic and problem solving. This anxiety, at the start of trainees' course, can be harmful to their test performance and can only exacerbate their lack of confidence. Provider-led preparation and private revision is seen as a solution. Ineson (2019) concludes that,

> '*The anxiety that many prospective students experience with the current testing arrangements means that their preparation for the* (numeracy) *test is likely to involve rote learning of algorithms* and *are likely to put some people off embarking on a teaching career*' (pp.20-21).

Literacy

My literature search (literacy 'skills test'; UK trainee teachers; QTS) found limited research on the Literacy PST beyond Hextall, Mahony & Menter (2001), Haworth (2002), Cajkler & Hislam (2003) and, finally, Riddick & English (2006). These research studies report how trainees (i) feel anxious, worried and stressed about the tests, (ii) have concerns, doubts and uncertainties over their difficulty, fearing rejection from failure, that (iii) affects their confidence and self-esteem.

Soon after the introduction of PSTs, Hextal et al. (2001) reported that there were '*major flaws in this… 'fast policy'*' (p.221) that left '*everyone affected by the initiative in a state of confusion or anxiety*' (p.237). The discrimination against disabled applicants, for example those with dyslexia (Riddick & English, 2006) being of particular concern. For Literacy, Cajkler and Hislam (2003) found that, despite pre-ITT trainees having,

> '*A significant amount of grammatical knowledge, they felt considerable anxiety about their level of understanding… (Although)…during the*(ir) *PGCE year, knowledge increased but anxiety remained high*' (p.161).

My experience of PSTs

On hearing that appointments at PST test centres were easier to get at the start of the ITE course year, I booked all three tests on the same day for Week 2. As a physics graduate with a career in I.T., I felt confident about passing Numeracy, reasonably so for I.C.T. but not for Literacy, my weakest subject at school. My rationale was, with limitless attempts possible at that time (2009), this was a chance simply to see what these tests were like and practise them under test conditions, but fully expecting to fail Literacy. And I thought that I would sit them during the initial lull before the first school experience kicked-in later that term.

As it happened, I passed all three tests, truly stunned at the success in Literacy. The time-dependant aspect (as described by Ineson (2018:15-16,18-19) for Numeracy, by Hextal et al. (2001:290) for Literacy] was, I found, quite stressful with little time to check answers and often in panic as the clock ran down. After back-to-back tests, I remember feeling quite exhausted and in need of a pint.

On reporting back to my ITE cohort, thinking my experience would encourage and de-stress them, it merely served to intensify collective anxieties. Conversely, their principle concerns were about numeracy and I.C.T. At the end of the course, I also noted how there were some teacher trainees with job offers that were dependent on passing outstanding PST(s).

David's story

David (in 2016, aged 17) recalls a quite different experience of the Literacy PST:

"I took the professional skills tests (QTS) between April and June in 2016... My plan being to have them completed ready for the university interview days; hoping having them completed would demonstrate how pro-active and determined I was to become a primary school teacher. At this time, the maximum amount of attempts allowed for these tests were three.

Before each test, I was very, very nervous. It felt like my entire dream career hinged on passing these exams. I knew that if I failed there would be no coming back. At least for the two year lockout period that you cannot retake the exams (but I knew after the two years my life would've moved on).

I was definitely more confident for the maths exam as that was always my stronger subject in school. I passed the mathematics exam on the first try... I know I passed... with a strong result.

But, unfortunately, I failed my English all three times... each one within only a few marks of the pass requirement. It was the spelling portion of the English exam that caught me out each time. In my opinion spelling words that no primary school student would ever use (and even in the case they did want to use them, let's be honest, we could just use the internet to check... I am still slightly frustrated about this). After I failed the English test for the third time I was very upset, (as) *ever since being a child, I have always wanted to be a teacher. Then, all of a sudden, this was no longer possible due to an arbitrary test. I was also more frustrated by the requirement for the English test as I had... (later passed)... three heavily English-based A-levels (Law, Psychology, and Sociology).*

The overall outcome being that, due to the failure, I had to give up my dream of becoming a primary school teacher. However, as they say, "when one door closes another one opens". I now have a fantastic career within [a National Bank], I did have a slight chuckle last year though when I received an email from the Department of Education letting me know they had removed the "three failure limit" and I could re-try whenever I wished.

I still get wound up to this day when I think about what was the point of a "three failure limit". The government is currently facing a severe lack of teaching support, even more critically with male primary school teachers! Why make the process to reduce this any harder? (especially when you already have to achieve a degree to become a teacher, is that not enough?). We let the population of England take an unlimited amount of driving tests yet because I couldn't spell "liaise" in an exam that hinged on my entire dream career becoming a reality, it was forcefully shut off to me."

I think David's frustration is self-evident and needs little further commentary.

Final thoughts

For me, passing each test so early during the PGCE meant three less hurdles to negotiate during the remaining academic year. But, in hindsight, it meant not having to revise as hard as others were, especially the grammatical knowledge, punctuation, spelling and comprehension skills I believe I lacked. This, however, seems insignificant when compared to David's 'dream career' ending outcome.

The DfE (2012) announced that, from April 2020, passing PSTs will no longer be required and that the responsibility to maintain standards would instead transfer to ITE course providers.

So, why has it taken the Department of Education so long to realise that PSTs have become '*too passé*' for purpose? Moreover, how many more Davids (or Davinas) will have been lost in the two years 2018-2020?

References

Cajkler, W. and Hislam J. (2003) 'Trainee teachers' grammatical knowledge: the tension between public expectation and individual competence', *Language Awareness,* 11(3), pp. 161-177.

Department for Education (2011) *Training our next generation of outstanding teachers: implementation plan.* Available at: https://assets.publishing.service.gov.uk/government/uploads/system/uploads/attachment_data/file/181154/DFE-00083-2011.pdf (Accessed: 28 October 2019).

Department for Education (2018) *Important changes to professional skills test.* Available at: http://sta.education.gov.uk (Accessed: 28 October 2019).

Department for Education (2019) *Skills test statistics.* Available at: http://sta.education.gov.uk/professional-skills-tests/skills-tests-statistics (Accessed 12 November 2019).

Haworth, A. (2002) 'Literacy tests for trainee teachers: shadows across the secondary classroom?', *Cambridge Journal of Education,* 32(3), pp. 289-302.

Hextall, I., Mahony, P. and Menter, I. (2001) 'Just testing? an analysis of the implementation of 'skills tests' for entry into the teaching profession in England', *Journal of Education for Teaching*, 27(3), pp. 221-239.

Ineson, G. (2019) 'What's the point of the professional skills test', In Watts, M., Luo, Y, Holder, D. M., Chen, S. Mohamed, M, Davis, G, Khawaja, A. (eds) *It's Education but not as you know it.* London: Brunel University, pp. 14-22.

Riddick, B. and English, E. (2006) 'Meeting the standards? Dyslexic students and the selection process for initial teacher training', *European Journal of Teacher Education,* 29 (2), pp. 203-222.

UCAS (2019) *Teacher training entry requirement in England.* Available at: https://www.ucas.com/postgraduate/teacher-training/train-teach-england/teacher-training-entry-requirements-england (Assessed: 28 October 2019).

The voice of educators and education students

Sichen Chen

Sichen is a 3rd year PhD student in the Education Department at Brunel University. With over 20 years of English language learning experiences, Sichen is super interested in exploring second/foreign language learning issues, especially about second language learners' difficulties while they are acquiring a new language. Therefore, Sichen is doing her PhD in investigating Chinese students' attitudes, values, and beliefs about English language learning.

The voice of educators and education students

What is the point of cognitive academic language learning approach (CALLA)?

Sichen Chen

I used to work as a teaching assistant in a private school in New York. I worked for eight hours each day from Monday to Friday. I was quite impressed by the program in this school which incorporated a variety of content areas including art, music, science, math, social studies. There were ten boys and seven girls, a total of seventeen students in my classroom, aged from four to five. Among them, five students from China had difficulties in listening and speaking English. That was one of the main reasons why I worked as an assistant teacher in the class. Besides me, there was one lead teacher and another assistant teacher. The classroom was decorated with students' colourful works and paintings. And there were three tables in the middle and a big carpet at the corner. Moreover, there were five centers, namely Block Center, Art Center, Library and Reading Center, Math Center, and Science Center for kids to play during the 'center time' (see Figure 1 & 2).

The voice of educators and education students

Figure 1

Figure 2

Everyday class began at 8:30 AM. After breakfast, the teacher guided students to do a warming-up activity in the classroom. All of them sat in a circle on a carpet, and they needed to figure out the date, month, weather, and count numbers. After that, the teacher played music and danced with the students. Then, it was learning time. For example, students learned two letters and learned how to write the letters with their fingers. Furthermore, they learned how to express the body parts. Next, at 10:30 AM, it was the happy hour. Kids could play at the playground for thirty minutes. After playing time, the tired kids went back to the classroom and sat on the carpet. The teacher used various materials, such as pictures, songs, and storybooks to help students learn new knowledge. After lunchtime, students had one hour to sleep. In the afternoon, it was 'center time'. All students could go to one center that they were interested in. Before the 'cleaning time', every student had five minutes to report what they found and learned while they were playing in the center. At last, the teacher gave the students some 'surprise' like stickers if they behaved well in the classroom. A happy day ended with many smiling faces.

The experience did not only consist of what I had seen, read, and heard, but also what I had done in the classroom. I learned about the Cognitive Academic Language Learning Approach (CALLA) lesson plan when I had my Master classes in New York. The CALLA lesson plan contains content-based knowledge, academic language and literacy, and the learning strategies instruction. I applied this learning strategy when I was working in this school. It appeared that the stages of CALLA could go through preparation, presentation, practice, self-evaluation and expansion. For the five English Language Learners in my class, they did not only need to learn the academic language but also the target knowledge. These kids recalled their background knowledge when answering questions. They learned knowledge during the circle time, and they practiced their knowledge during the center time.

One of my students left a deep impression on me. He was called Jacky (nickname), and he was five years old. He came here from China when he was four years old. Thus, he had difficulty in listening and speaking English. Jacky could only understand and speak simple English, so he always sat alone and did not listen to the teacher. I knew Jacky was able to understand and speak Chinese well. Therefore, I translated English into Chinese and then asked him to read English after me. I was assigned to help Jacky learn English knowledge from the class. First, I spoke to him in Chinese. He was surprised and pleased that I could speak Chinese. Thus, we got closer and closer. According to the teacher's directions, I translated them into Chinese so that Jacky could understand. Then, I taught Jacky how to speak in English. For example, the teacher asked students to show the body parts they knew. I asked Jacky to show me first and speak it in Chinese, then I told him the English words of each body part. Jacky would read after me. Moreover, if Jacky pronounced the words accurately, I would say "Great! Good job!" to enhance his confidence.

In my opinion, the effective teaching approach should include the specific objectives, the scientific procedures and teaching strategies, the tacit cooperation between teachers and students, the active interaction between them, and the positive results of teaching and learning. The CALLA teaching approach is one of the appropriate teaching strategies applied in the classroom, especially in an English language learning class.

Abdirazak Osman

My Name is Abdirazak Osman and I am currently a second year Doctoral Researcher undertaking EdD. My professional background is Youth Work but my intellectual interest lies in the highly contested epistemological dimensions of Vocational Education and Training (VET) and the perceptions of young people who pursue these work-related courses.

Vocational education and training (VET): skills training or individual formation?

Abdirazak Osman

Since the Ancient Greeks, there have been different conceptions of education and indeed Aristotle enquired whether the purpose of education should focus on 'livelihoods', 'promote virtues' or advance 'higher studies' (Armitage et al., 2003: 23); conceptions of education that modern philosophers of education reappropriate as *vocational*, *civic* and *liberal* education. Liberal and civic conceptions of education have acquired a stable epistemological status, whereas vocational education has evolved as elusive and sometimes polarising forms of knowledge amongst philosophers of education. Vocational education is always contrasted in liberal education in a more reductive and dichotomic fashion by using traditional distinctions between teleological and instrumental, cognitive and practical, academic and vocational, concept and skill, as though these human experiences are neatly segmented in reality. Peters (1972) believed that educational programmes focusing on instrumental values undermine the real purpose of education, which is the introduction of educational experiences and practices that are valuable in themselves. This VET epistemological instability permeated into societal and policy making consciousness and impacted on its curriculum design as a form of knowledge as well as its long term, ideal purpose – *skills* and *individual* formation.

Although VET scholarship has attempted to establish the status and the structure of VET epistemology, it unintentionally created two incongruous propositions regarding the purpose of VET enterprise. The first argument sees VET values through the economic rationality as though its sole purpose is to satisfy the desires of the labour market. The second argument sees VET values through the holistic formation of individual growth initiating an autonomous and productive citizen. On the surface, these propositions appear to be complementary narratives advancing VET theory of knowledge with an integrated and progressive curriculum. However, questions about the long-term contribution of VET provisions to individual subjectification, skills formation and employment participation remain. This concise chapter is a prelude to my doctoral enquiry examining the extent that VET programmes contribute to young peoples' life projects; whilst unifying these dichotomic formulations and propose that the VET enterprise can be both a skills and individual formation experience, developing an individual with social, civic and economic capabilities.

As I have articulated above, there are two distinct VET models – *skills or individual* formation - which have different teleology regarding curriculum content, individual cultivation and employment outcomes. The prioritisation of mere *skill* training without *individual* formation brought lots of criticism from the *liberal-vocationalist* tradition, a tradition that advocates the integration of liberal and vocational education (Winch, 2000; Fuller and Unwin, 2003). These critics question any VET enterprise solely emphasising economic productivity and reducing an entire educational experience to its instrumental values, while unveiling that the societal and policy makers' presuppositions of VET programmes is to remedy the skills shortage in the labour market. In this regard, VET curriculum prioritises 'the ability to perform narrowly circumscribed tasks in the work place' (Winch, 2012: 60). Winch argues that this reductive model of vocational education lacks the space for personal development and growth, for it is conditional to pursue job-related qualification specified within occupational sector frameworks. Similarly, Fuller and Unwin (2003) proposed *restrictive* and *expansive* models of Apprenticeship programmes. The restrictive model prioritises the *skills* gained through a demonstration of narrow and prescribed performances and competences without employment of reflexive knowledge. In other words, this restrictive VET model does not accommodate three domains of educational purposes that Biesta (2015) called qualification, socialisation and subjectification for holistic individual formation. This restrictive model prepares *workers* at best, or is merely social inclusion policy that does not even guarantee employment but is nevertheless used and abused by politicians to make mass youth unemployment statistics respectable. What is contradictory in this debate is that albeit British governments of different persuasions represent VET enterprise as a magic key unlocking skills formation and economic prosperity, the culture of society and educationalists at large see VET provisions as a mere training for specific occupational tasks. Moreover, vocational education is linked to a *practical knowledge* which is construed as mere skills training rather than theoretically informed knowledge. In this traditionalist definition of practical knowledge, the term *skill* is reduced to a situational judgement or performance of certain tasks at the expense of a broad-based VET curriculum (Winch, 2012). This reductive way of conceptualising practical knowledge as a *skill* is unique to an English speaking world, an attitude that makes it difficult to establishing any status for VET project.

As a result, these liberal vocationalists advocate a holistic VET curriculum integrating Biesta's domains of education and creating space for individual development and growth. Fuller and Unwin's (2003) *expansive* model prioritises *individual* development through knowledge-based curriculum integrating theoretical and occupational contents, while creating a space for social and civic development. According to Brockmann et al. (2010: 113), any VET curriculum forming individual capabilities should be based on a broad 'occupational knowledge and competences as well as general and civic education'. This model prepares a *citizen* possessing all the capabilities required to become a fully functioning individual. The current British VET curriculum and policy documents have so far fallen short in recognising the absence of knowledge-based VET provision that integrates general education and occupational contents. The closest that English VET comes to this realisation was Wolf's report (2011) commissioned by the coalition government, but the recommendations of this report did not go far enough in transforming the current performative VET system. The Continental VET system is regarded as an ideal model that prioritises an *individual*, and then provides the tools and skills that person requires to become a responsible, productive member of an occupation. This broad conception of VET programme integrates theoretical and practical knowledge of the occupation while promoting social and civic instruments necessary to become a capable person. This model is not only a skills formation enterprise, but it is a character building experience generating citizens who can function autonomously within their occupation and society.

Although these two conceptions of VET enterprise reflect contemporary academic and to a certain extent educational policy discourses, they are normally articulated in a way that is distant from the reality of the young people pursuing this vocational, work-related learning. These young people do not dissociate *skills* from the individual, occupational and social contexts in which they are utilised, and thus are not interested in the differential modalities of VET provisions; their concern is how far their work-related vocational courses enable their life projects both intrinsically and instrumentally. As a result, this doctoral project will interrogate these conceptions of VET enterprise through the voices of young people by explicating how they identify, plan and fulfil their life projects. What agential actions contributed to the acquisition of their vocational knowledge? And how far do vocational courses contribute or constrain the fulfilment of their life project? *Life project* refers to the ambitions and aspirations that the young people have, whereas *agential action* refers to both contemplative and concrete actions that young people undertake to chart the journey of their life project. *Vocational knowledge* refers to the acquisition of both practical and theoretical knowledge that facilitates the achievement of young peoples' life projects.

In relation to a theoretical framework, this study draws from the human *capability approach* (2009), which has two unique benefits regarding VET research. Firstly, the capability approach prioritises the individual formation, freedom and well-being, which is different from the exclusive economic rationality of *human capital* theory. Secondly, the capability approach is an evaluative instrument enabling researchers to understand the contributions of VET programmes to young peoples' life projects (Powell and McGrath, 2019). Although some proponents of the capability approach proposed a list of capabilities that national and international education systems should legislate for every human-being to achieve, this study will not essentialise any preformed capability dimensions but use research participants' aspirations and priorities as a guiding principle to understand what is valuable for their instrumental and intrinsic functioning (achievements), and how far the decisions of their life projects, including the selection of vocational courses, contributed or constrained their valuable functioning. One of the challenges of the *capability* conceptis its abstractive nature, which can be regarded as *potential* or *becoming*, rather than an objective phenomenon. One way of reifying the capability concept and overcoming its abstract ontology is the evaluation of young peoples' capabilities regarding the achievement of their aspirations, be it the acquisition of musical skills, securing employment in the music industry, etcetera. Although this research theoretically converges with Powell and McGrath's (2019) study in vocational education in South Africa, the divergence is that current study examines the fallacious bifurcation of skills and individual formation in VET curriculum theory, which hitherto did not receive enough attention in the VET literature; rather than poverty dimensions in which the above study focused.

In conclusion, one durable complication of VET programmes is that VET curriculum is not only problematically compared with liberal education, but within VET forms of knowledge, there are *restrictive-* skill training curriculum - associated with English speaking world, and *expansive* curriculum with its knowledge-rich content prevalent in continental Europe. If the educationalists of English speaking world want to shift the attitude of employers and society in general from the dichotomic conceptions of VET project, integration of practical and theoretical knowledge of VET content should be universalised to initiate future generations with technical and cognitive capabilities; therefore, making VET programmes both *skills*and *individual* formation enterprise.

References

Armitage, A. et al. (2013) *Teaching and Training in post-compulsory Education.* Berkshire: OUP.

Biesta, G. (2015) 'What is education for? On good education, teacher judgement and educational professionalism', *European Journal of Education,* 50(1), pp. 75-87.

Brockmann, M., Clarke, L. and Winch, C. (2010) 'The apprenticeship framework in England: a new beginning or a continuing sham?', *Journal of Education and Work,* 23(2), pp. 111-127.

Fuller, A. and Unwin, L. (2003) 'Learning as apprentices in the contemporary UK workplace: creating and managing expansive and restrictive participation', *Journal of Vocational education and Training,* 63(3), pp. 55-71.

Peters, R. S. (1972) 'Education and educated man', in Dearden, R. F., Hirst, P. H. and Peters, R. S. (eds.) *Education and the Development of Reason.* London: Routledge and Keagon Paul.

Powell, L. and McGrath, S. (2019) *Skills for Human Development: Transforming Vocational Education and Training.* Oxon: Routledge.

Sen, A. (2009) *The Idea of Justice.* London: Penguin Books.

Winch, C. (2012) 'Research in vocational education and training', *British Journal of Educational Studies,* 60(1), pp. 53-63.

Winch, C. (2000) *Education, Work and Social Capital: Towards a New Conception of Vocational Education.* London: Routledge.

Wolf, A. (2011) *Review of Vocational Education - the Wolf Report.* London: Department of Education. Available at: https://assets.publishing.service.gov.uk/government/uploads/system/uploads/attachment_data/file/180504/DFE-00031-2011.pdf .

The voice of educators and education students

Jawaher Almutairi

MA in TESOL, MA in Counseling and Ph.D. in Education. I always believed that teaching is a privilege & responsibility! I have expertise in teaching English in higher education and in coaching students towards achieving their goals. My goal as an educator is to impart a passion for education within the classroom.

Intercultural perspectives in multicultural education

Jawaher Almutairi

The biggest deficiency that teachers in my region struggle with is effective intercultural communication with students who are not the majority group of upper-middle-class, Caucasian, Southern Baptists speaking perfect English. We tend to judge prejudicially darker complexioned Hindus, Muslims, and Africans who come from lower socioeconomic strata as being more unintelligent and undisciplined than 'regular' students. Their religious needs are discounted in the classroom, such as Muslim requests for prayer five times per day. The consequence of this bias is that these students are disproportionately placed into special education unnecessarily at high rates. Studies reveal that 15% of dark-skinned students have a risk ratio of 2.28 times higher than whites for placement after being labeled with 'emotional' and 'intellectual' disabilities (Harry & Klingner, 2014, p. 2). As an intercultural educator, I desire to significantly rectify the lack of multicultural communication in my school district within 12 months.

Therefore, I designed a lesson plan which consists of a 5-slide PowerPoint presentation discussing biases and strategies to integrate multicultural education into school districts. Participants will be given a handout to reflect on unconscious biases against minority students. Those who score highest on "I teach to give and receive love" will likely feel the most anger and disillusionment with multicultural classrooms (Grant & Sleeter, 2011, p. 7). A discussion will occur about multicultural/bilingual books and strategies to hire more bilingual teachers. Research shows that children of darker complexion are academically damaged by the dominant educational culture as they rarely see role models of colour in educational literature or as leaders (Soule, 2012). Other ideas include an introduction to multicultural music to depart from traditional Anglo chalkboard-testing models (Anderson & Campbell, 2011).

Intercultural communication concepts represent the fundamental theories for examination by students. Identifying areas in which students can extract common principles and practices among speakers of multiple language and traditions become the primary educational activity for study (Grant, 2011). The process prepares students for interacting with multiple demographics of student populations, particularly in academic environments experiencing significant changes in enrollment from immigrant populations. While many school districts currently possess 50% of minority students, language continues to be a significant obstacle preventing many students from achieving maximum academic successes (Harry & Klinger, 2014). Therefore, the study of intercultural communication aims to reduce the efficiency of such obstacles by dispelling myths associated with certain minority population's ability to learn and interact with others, including the persistent need for special education and the abundance of emotional and cognitive deficiencies.

The lesson plan for intercultural communication includes 1) mandatory personal reflection by each student, 2) examination of theoretical and practical concepts regarding multiculturalism in academic environments, and 3) practical applications recommended for strategies in academic and professional environments to promote effective intercultural communication. The course lesson plan asks each student to complete a cultural self-assessment exercise; the activity requires each participant to reflect upon personal cultural beliefs and traditions. Urging students to engage in a theoretical and practical examination of belief systems increases the prospect of students seeking to learn about ideas outside their current perspective. However, self-reflection remains the primary exercise necessary for implementation before students deriving conclusive findings regarding intercultural communication theory.

The self-reflection process provides answers to questions concerning individual identity, including belonging to protected classes of gender, race, and ethnicity. Several questions concern the student's behaviors regarding cultural traditions, including topics for daily discussion, the perceived difference between public and private activities, and how the individuals perceive particular forms of communication in the presence of people from multiple demographics.

A subsequent intercultural awareness activity provides students with the opportunity to interact with others from a different culture. The activity requires the participating student body to be divided into three distinct categories. The exemplary paradigm divides students by ethnic and religious groups: Latinos, Muslims, and Africans. However, the activity is not exclusive only to these groups and can be applied by those belonging to other ethnic or religious groups, as well as additional categories like gender and age (Soule, 2012). Each group receives a printed handout explaining the cultural facts and traditions present among the other two groups. After each group gains the opportunity to study other cultures, the three groups form a larger group and interact with individuals outside of their group for an extended period. Subsequently, the students break into the three distinct groups once again to discuss what they learned about intercultural communication, and the new information is different from pre-conceived perspectives. The three groups reform one final time to share concluding findings with the entire mass of students.

Interpersonal communication helps students understand the working application of chosen identity and how to relate to other students from different backgrounds. The lesson plan aims to dispel many of the myths associated with teaching diverse groups of students and strives to provide a practical method for promoting effective interpersonal communication for all students. The lesson plan seeks to provide students from all backgrounds with the opportunity to experience an academic environment aided by diverse populations and ideas.

The voice of educators and education students

Priya Jaswal

Priya Jaswal is a postgraduate student at Brunel University London. She will graduate with a master's degree from The College of Business, Arts and Social Sciences. Priya's paper evaluates sociological explanations of social class differences in educational achievement.

Class and educational achievement

Priya Jaswal

Introduction

In this paper, I will assess the view that working-class underachievement in education is the result of home circumstances and family background (Smith and Noble, 1995). There are two dominant ways of looking at the extent to which educational achievement differs between social groups (Fuller, 1984). The interactionist sociologist, Fuller (1984), views factors inside the education system, in particular, teacher-pupil relationships and the curriculum, as responsible for class differences. However, I follow Jerrim (2013) and argue that social class differences in educational attainment are a result of factors outside the education system, such as material and cultural deprivation.

There are key explanations of class differences in educational achievement. In particular, I will explore how low income reduces the likelihood of pupils having access to resources that can directly help students to succeed in the education system, for example, materials for school (Smith and Noble, 1995). Then, I will examine variation in educational attainment in terms of cultural differences.

Bourdieu and Passeron (1977) view working-class culture as failing to provide the necessary attributes for educational success, and consequently claim that the working-class are culturally deprived.

Material deprivation

Jerrim (2013) argues that certain children have less money than others and so are not able to make the most of their educational opportunities. For example, in a study of the effects of poverty on schooling, Smith and Noble (1995) list the 'barriers to learning' which can result from low income, and found that if families are unable to afford school trips, school uniforms, transport to and from school, classroom materials and, in some cases, school textbooks, this can lead to children being bullied, isolated and stigmatised. Whilst state education is technically free in Britain, supplementary costs can be considerable and excluding for some families (Jerrim, 2013). However, less in recent years, the Government of the United Kingdom has attempted to reduce the material disadvantages faced by working-class pupils through positive discrimination (Erickson, McDonald and Elder, 2009). This takes the form of programmes of compensatory education that plough more resources into poorer areas (Erickson, McDonald and Elder, 2009). An illustration of this in England occurred when the Conservative government in the 1990s allocated up to twenty-five per cent more money to local authorities in less affluent areas (Erickson, McDonald and Elder, 2009). Furthermore, the introduction of Educational Action Zones by the Labour government in the late 1990s was also an attempt to raise standards by making up for the effects of material deprivation (Erickson, McDonald and Elder, 2009). This suggests that all of Conservative's and Labour's educational policies are designed to fit into a wider social mobility strategy in which it was hoped that there would be equality of opportunity for disadvantaged children

(Erickson, McDonald and Elder, 2009).

Sullivan (2001) claims that material inequality outside school has a negative impact on pupils' experiences inside the school. Research by Washbrook and Waldfogel (2010) for The Sutton Trust looked at the effect of material deprivation on the scores of five-year-olds in vocabulary tests. They discovered that thirty-one per cent of the difference in scores between children from middle-income and low-income families was explained by material deprivation (Washbrook and Waldfogel, 2010). This highlights that high achieving students from the most advantaged family backgrounds are ahead of their counterparts in the least advantaged households by the age of five (Washbrook and Waldfogel, 2010). As a result, low income increases the likelihood of students falling behind in their school work (Sullivan, 2001). Nevertheless, underclass theorists, such as Marsland (1996), see working-class culture as failing to provide the necessary attributes for educational success and therefore argue that the working-class are culturally deprived. Research by Goodman and Gregg (2010) for the Joseph Rowntree Foundation used data from four longitudinal studies (The Millennium Cohort Study, the Avon Longitudinal Study of Parents and Children, the Longitudinal Study of Young People in England, and the Children of the British Cohort Study) to investigate the link between poverty and low achievement in children from birth through secondary school years (Goodman and Gregg, 2010). They did not attribute low attainment entirely to material factors, but identified cultural deprivation (for instance, lack of parents involvement in schooling, the poor value placed on education by the adult carers) and increased levels of negative behaviour by the children (for instance, antisocial behaviour, smoking and truancy) as the most important of all (Goodman and Gregg, 2010). This signifies that the working-class place too much emphasis on enjoying themselves and living in the moment rather than on putting in the hard work and making the sacrifices necessary for educational success (Marsland, 1996).

Cultural deprivation theory

Bourdieu and Passeron (1977) suggested that middle and upper-class culture (cultural capital) is as valuable in educational terms as material wealth (economic capital). Schools, it is argued, are middle-class institutions run by a small, high-class minority (Bourdieu and Passeron, 1977). The forms of knowledge and values that children from these classes possess are developed further and rewarded by the education system (Bourdieu and Passeron, 1977). Working-class and minority ethnic children may lack these qualities and so do not have the same chances to succeed (Bourdieu and Passeron, 1977). In 1998, Sullivan (2001) carried out surveys to investigate the impact of class on cultural capital and achievement. Her research focused on students approaching the school-leaving age in four schools in England and received questionnaire data from a total of four hundred sixty-five pupils (Sullivan, 2001). Sullivan (2001) asked questions about the involvement of the children in cultural activities (for example, reading books, attending theatres and concerts) and the parents' own educational achievements. She found that parental income helps to boost the educational performance of children independent of cultural factors (Sullivan, 2001). This highlights that cultural capital is the pursuit of conspicuous academic achievement by both parents and children of higher social classes (Bourdieu and Passeron, 1977). Nonetheless, cultural deprivation theory sounds deterministic: educational success and failure seems to be entirely determined by the background of pupils, which gives pupils little apparent control over their own achievement (Fuller, 1984). It is clear that not all working-class pupils live up to underachievement

(Fuller, 1984). Research by Fuller (1984) found that the group of black working-class girls in her study managed to use their rejection by the school to motivate them to be successful, and they were able to overcome the barriers put in their path to achieve high grades (Fuller, 1984). This signifies that rather than a self-fulfilling prophecy taking place, students can rebel against the low expectations of the school (Fuller, 1984).

Bernstein (1971) points out that a particular aspect of culture – speech – shapes educational achievement. He distinguishes two types of speech pattern: restricted codes, which involve simpler use of language, and elaborated codes, which involve more complex use of language (Bernstein, 1971). In education, elaborated codes are necessary for exam success in many subjects (Bernstein, 1971). Being socialised in households that largely use restricted codes holds back working-class children in the education system, making it more difficult for them to achieve academic success (Bernstein, 1971). Feinstein (2003) used data from the National Child Development Study to examine the effects of cultural and other factors in shaping educational achievement. He noted that financial deprivation (having poorer parents) had some effect on achievement, but that cultural deprivation was much more important (Feinstein, 2003). The overriding factor was the extent to which parents were able to use their cultural capital to give their children a head start (Feinstein, 2003). The working-class parents tended to have low-level educational qualifications themselves and a poor understanding of how children could be stimulated to learn in pre-school years (Feinstein, 2003). They were not able to use their own educational experience to incorporate learning activities into their children's play (Feinstein, 2003). This highlights that working-class families lack the ability to provide a stimulating home learning environment, thus children possess less of the cultural capital useful for success in the education system (Bernstein, 1971). Nonetheless, the New Labour government of 1997 challenged whether there really were such big cultural differences between social classes in the contemporary world (Glendinning, Powell and Rummery, 2002). One of the most well-established initiatives, Sure Start, aimed to reduce social exclusion and promote equality of opportunity, by providing a number of measures, including additional pre-school education to tackle cultural deprivation which places working-class children at a disadvantage before they even start school, and bring together a range of support services in disadvantaged communities (Glendinning, Powell and Rummery, 2002). This suggests that educational policies aimed directly at reducing class inequalities may make working-class children feel as confident as middle-class children in a school environment, as individuals possess more of the cultural capital useful for success in the education system (Glendinning, Powell and Rummery, 2002).

Conclusion

This paper has explored that social class differences in educational achievement are a result of factors outside the education system, such as material and cultural deprivation (Smith and Noble, 1995). For example, working-class students may have a lack of resources to purchase goods, such as classroom materials, as well as being deprived of cultural capital that can give an individual advantage in life (Glendinning, Powell and Rummery, 2002). Nevertheless, less in recent years, governments have attempted to reduce the material and cultural disadvantages faced by working-class pupils in the form of compensatory education (Erickson, McDonald and Elder, 2009). This is demonstrated in ways such as Sure Start, launched in 1998 and the introduction of Educational Action Zones by the Labour government in the late 1990s (Glendinning, Powell and Rummery,

2002). Nevertheless, class is not the only social division that has an impact on educational attainment; ethnicity and gender is also important (Smith and Noble, 1995).

Acknowledgements

I would like to take this opportunity to first and foremost thank all the staff in the Department of Education and Academic Skills (ASK) who have inspired the writing of this paper over the months. I would also like to thank my fellow peers for the advice and confidence they have endlessly provided throughout the years.

References

Bernstein, B. (1971) *Class, Codes and Control*. London: Routledge and Kegan Paul.

Bourdieu, P. and Passeron, J. (1977) *Reproduction in Education, Society and Culture*. London: Sage.

Erickson, L. D., McDonald, S. and Elder, G. H. (2009) 'Informal mentors and education: complementary or compensatory resources?', *Sociology of Education*, 82 (4), pp. 344 – 367.

Feinstein, L. (2003) 'Inequality in the early cognitive development of British children in the 1970 cohort', *Economica*, 70 (277), pp. 73 – 98.

Fuller, M. (1984) 'Black girls in a London comprehensive', in Deem, R. (ed.) *Schooling for Women's Work*. London: Routledge.

Glendinning, C., Powell, M. A., Rummery, K. (2002) *Partnerships, New Labour and the Governance of Welfare*. Bristol: Policy Press.

Goodman, A. and Gregg, P. (2010) *Poorer Children's Educational Attainment: How Important are Attitudes and Behaviour?* York: Joseph Rowntree Foundation.

Jerrim, J. (2013) *Family Background and Access to 'High Status' Universities*. London: The Sutton Trust.

Marsland, D. (1996) *Welfare or Welfare State?* Basingstoke: Macmillan.

Smith, T. and Noble, M. (1995) *Poverty and Schooling in the 1990s*. London: Child Poverty Action Group.

Sullivan, A. (2001) 'Cultural capital and educational attainment', *Sociology*, 35 (4), pp. 893 – 912.

Washbrook, E. and Waldfogel, J. (2010) *Low Income and Early Cognitive Development in the UK*. London: The Sutton Trust.

The voice of educators and education students

Carolina Akinyi Nyakila

I was born to Christian parents in 1980 in Tanzania, a country situated in East Africa. I am one of eight children and the 6th born in our family. I spent most of my time in boarding school in Kenya between the age of 9 and 18 years old and achieved certificates of primary and secondary education, and certificates in netball and class prefect. At the age of 19 and 20 years I achieved certificates in computing packaging and secretarial studies. In 2001 I migrated to England, United Kingdom where I am now settled. Since being in England, I have attained Certificates in Dental Nursing, Access to Higher Education Teacher Training and recognition for The Nationwide Awards for Voluntary Endeavors as part of the work I did as Miss Kenya UK for 2 years. I am a mother of one daughter and currently pursuing an undergraduate degree in education at Brunel University London and working with young people at my church on a voluntary basis.

Is the government doing enough to promote good oral health in children?

Carolina Akinyi Nyakila

'Oral health is a part of general health and wellbeing and contributes to the development of a healthy child and school readiness' (Gov.UK, 2018). According to World Health Organization (2018), good oral health is being in a state free from constant recurring facial and mouth pains, tooth loss, tooth decay, gum disease, oral and throat cancer, oral decay and any other illness that restricts an individual from smiling, masticating, biting and psychosocial wellbeing. Studies show that the most common oral disease that affects children in England is tooth decay. Statistics show that approximately 24.7% of 5- year olds suffer from tooth decay and about 25,000 young children are hospitalised every year as a result (Gov.UK, 2018; BBC, 2014).

Causes of poor oral health

Regular consumption of food and drinks containing a lot of sugar makes the chances of having tooth decay very high. Secondly, so does insufficient access to fluoride, including embarking on tooth brushing late and irregular brushing of teeth without or with very little fluoride toothpaste. Thirdly, deprivation - including low income, lack of education, unemployment and environmental circumstances - can affect a child's normal growth including their teeth (Gov.UK, 2018). On the other hand, the BBC (2014) argues that most children have poor oral health given the fact that parents have been neglecting children's gums and milk teeth, and they will eventually fall out.

Effects of poor oral health in children in education

Research conducted in North West Hospitals entailing tooth extraction in children found that 26% of children had missed at least three days of school following dental infection, pain and general dental problems. This in turn affected 41% of parents and guardians who were in employment, as they had to take time off work, hence creating financial constraints (Gov.UK, 2018). Furthermore, 38% of children who suffered with dental pain could not sleep throughout the night and school performance was affected as a result (Gov.UK, 2018).

According to Poulos (2015), children with poor oral health struggle to learn because of lack of mental concentration and sharpness. Moreover, these children are disturbed mentally and emotionally as they are unable to keep up with the rest of the class. Thus, they may isolate themselves from the other children and consequently suffer socially which could lead to low moods. Additionally, children who are unable to masticate when eating then swallow their food, which radically interferes with their body's ability to gain weight hence low self-esteem due to their weight loss (Poulos, 2015).

Studies indicate that children with missing front teeth suffer from social development in that, word formation becomes inadequate and the children become shy and avoid socialising with their peers. Additionally, children with infected teeth can have ear infection that affects their ability to hear in class. The tooth infection can further incur an abscess (a swelling found in the body tissue and contains pus), and sinus infections leading to irritableness, anxiousness and isolation which could hinder children's academic performance and school attendance. Furthermore, children with untreated dental caries lived a life of poor oral health and in some cases were underweight by 80% of their ideal normal weight (Sheiham, 2013).

According to Ceatus Media Group LLC (2019), children with decayed and missing teeth may end up with misaligned or crooked permanent teeth, causing difficulties in maintaining good oral hygiene and may also foster distorted facial appearance hence low self-esteem and social isolation.

Again, Ceatus Media Group LLC (2019), informs us that children who suck their thumbs following eruption of permanent teeth, which is around five years old, normally have speech problems, thus, making it difficult for the children to express themselves in class and around their peers, hence social isolation and lack of self-confidence. In addition, thumb sucking in children causes misalignment of the jaws and roof of their mouth, known as the palate. This may affect children's facial appearance and make them self-conscious with feelings of inadequacy resulting in low mood, low self-esteem and social exclusion at school.

Tongue thrusting is another factor that affects children's oral health, resulting in interference with their education. Putting immense pressure on the tongue against the lips causes tongue thrusting that may consequently lead to protrusion of teeth (Ceatus Media Group LLC, 2019). Mosaic Rehabilitation (2019), reinforces this in saying that children affected by tongue thrusting have problems with their speech and appearance due to drooling and tongue protrusion which may result in social isolation, low mood and speech problems, and in turn affect their school performance and attendance.

Studies also show that parents who suffer from oral health diseases such as tooth decay and periodontal disease also known as gum disease, most certainly witness their children struggle with similar oral health conditions due to bacteria found in the parent's mouth and passed on to their children by way of kissing and sharing food. For this reason, the children struggle to stay calm in class and may not concentrate in their learning. In the event that they are taken to see the dentist, their school attendance is affected (Ceatus Media Group LLC, 2019).

Government strategies to combat poor oral health in children

The government has put in place supervised tooth brushing programmes in schools and nurseries where learners are taught to brush their teeth from a tender age and are encouraged to brush their teeth at home. Early years settings provide managers and the workforce with oral health training so as to impart and apply that knowledge to children in their settings. These institutions also have policies around healthy eating (Gov.UK, 2017). For instance, provision of free school meals comprising a full balance diet and fruits at break times instead of sugary snacks.

Children from the age of 0 to 6 years are encouraged to brush their teeth at least twice a day using family fluoride toothpaste that has 1350 to 1500 parts per million of fluoride in order to reach the maximum prevention of tooth decay. A pea size amount of toothpaste is encouraged for 3 to 6-year olds while a smear size is encouraged for 0 to 3 year olds (Gov.UK, 2017). High-risk areas where deprived children and young people settle are given priority by providing them free toothbrushes and toothpastes. Health visitors supports this programme and make sure there is a smooth continuation of messages among professionals (Gov.UK, 2017).

The government has also issued targeted community fluoride varnish programmes where children especially in high risk locations are visited in schools and early years settings and fluoride varnish is applied to their teeth twice a year. Moreover, promotions of good oral health messages are given in these settings and at dental appointments (Gov.UK, 2017).

Another government strategy is the water fluoridation scheme where fluoride is added in water to decrease any chances of having tooth decay and to prevent its severity. Water fluoridation has had successful results given statistics showing a rise in figures where 55% of very young children are no longer being hospitalized for tooth extractions in fluoridated regions compared to areas that are not fluoridated. Statistics also reveal that 28% of five-year olds in fluoridated regions are less likely to suffer from tooth decay compared to those in non-fluoridated locations. This intervention has worked successful in England for 60 years (Gov.UK, 2017).

Gov.UK, (2017) states that dental teams are trained to provide oral health advice to children. They also encourage parents to make dental appointments as soon as their children's teeth erupt, normally at about six months old. Where healthier diets need fostering, the dental team refers parents to organisations such as Change4Life (2019) that has a 'Be food smart app' that gives parents an awareness of hidden sugars and a way to minimise or prevent increased sugar consumption.

The government has also entrusted health visitors, school

nurses, GPs, paediatricians, general practice nurses, midwives and pharmacists with a duty to give oral health advice as a part of the healthy child programme (Gov.UK, 2017). Furthermore, the government has a voluntary sector where free parenting programmes entailing oral health is issued. The voluntary sector also provides the early years workforce with continuous professional development training in oral health in order to combat poor oral health in children (Gov.UK, 2017).

Moreover, specialist societies are available to ensure that all children receive a high standard of care by supporting children's oral health, managing, developing and advertising oral health initiatives and very good evidence, guidelines and clinical procedures for health care professionals and the public and engaging with the public through patient information leaflets (Gov.UK, 2017). In addition, Royal Colleges provide professional development and pre- and post-graduate education for dental and child health professionals and give policies and guidelines to inform the public and professionals (Gov.UK, 2017). Finally, consultants in public health partner with the NHS England, Health Education England, Local Professionals' Network and Local Authority Public Health teams to give an enhanced dental health upon one's entire life course, providing every child a favourable beginning in life (Gov. UK, 2017).

Conclusion

It is evident that the government is doing so much to combat poor oral health in children. The strategies in place has helped reduce poor oral health in various regions across England. However, poor oral health still remains a significant problem given that children in England are still eating an extra 2,800 sugar cubes per annum, meaning the daily recommended intake is exceeded by more than a double which in turn impacts on children in education.

References

> Ceatus Media Group LLC (2019) *Red flags to poor oral health in your child.* Available at: https://www.yourdentistryguide.com/children-poor-oral-health/ (Accessed: 07 May 2019).
>
> NHS.UK (2019) *Food labels: find out what to look out for on food labels and make healthier choices for the family.* Available at: https://www.nhs.uk/change4life/food-facts/food-labels (Accessed: 07 May 2019).
>
> NHS.UK (2019) *Lower sugar drinks for kids.* Available at: https://www.nhs.uk/change4life/food-facts/healthier-snacks-for-kids/lower-sugar-drinks-for-kids-stop-tooth-decay (Accessed: 07 May 2019).
>
> NHS.UK (2019) *5 a day: all you need to know about 5 a day for the whole family – portion, sizes, top tips and what fruit and veg count.* Available at: https://www.nhs.uk/change4life/food-facts/five-a-day (Accessed: 07 May 2019).
>
> GOV.UK (2018) *Child oral health: applying All Our Health.* Available at: https://www.gov.uk/government/publications/child-oral-health-applying-all-our-health/child-oral-health-applying-all-our-health (Accessed: 07 May 2019).
>
> GOV.UK (2017) *Health matters: child dental health.* Available at: https://www.gov.uk/government/publications/health-matters-child-dental-health/health-matters-child-dental-health (Accessed: 07 May 2019).
>
> Mosaic Rehabilitation (2019) *Specialising in physical, occupational and speech therapy.* Available at: https://www.mosaicrehabmt.com/tongue-thrust-and-speech-development/ (Accessed: 07 May

2019).

Poulos, T. (2015) *Children's oral health: establish good habits early.* Available at: https://www.alive.com/health/children%C2%92s-oral-health/ (Accessed: 07 May 2019).

Sheiham, A. (2013) *Oral health-general health: a common risk factor approach.* Available at: http://www.eadph.org/congresses/18th/Oral %20Health-General%20Health%20CRFA%20Sheiham.pdf (Accessed: 07 May 2019).

World Health Organization (2018) *Oral health: general information.* Available at: https://www.who.int/oral_health/en/ (Accessed: 07 May 2019).

The voice of educators and education students

Monia Al-Farsi

I'm a Doctoral Researcher in the Department of Education at Brunel University. I have experience across the areas of academic fields like teaching IT courses at undergraduate levels, developing, reviewing, updating of syllabus and IT courses, providing students with academic advice and supervising graduation projects. Bedside my teaching duties, I have undertaken Student Affairs Deanship duties, which encompass areas including Admission and Registration, On-the-Job Training, Counselling and Graduates Follow-up, Housing, Student Activities, and Graduation. My PhD research is focusing on the e-Learning at the higher education institutions in my country Oman. My research interests are Information System, Social Sciences, Education, eLearning, M-Leaning, Project Management, Digital Technology and Technology Challenges.

Can e-learning make them skillful?

Monia Al-Farsi

Introduction

'Learning' is one of the most important aspects that strongly reflect the advancement of society. With the presence of information technology and its development nowadays, the relationship between information technology and learning has changed and is growing significantly. Therefore, the name 'electronic-learning' is given to the use of electronic methods or applications to deliver better, easier and more flexible education to students.

In education, with a focus on employability and skills, many studies and information have examined the importance of skill improvement of higher education students because, in most cases, the skills of graduates do not meet the expectations of employers.

From my work experience as an academic in one of Oman's Higher Education Colleges, most of the courses that are taught in the college are dedicated to acquiring knowledge (theory and practice), by establishing objectives and assessment procedures, with an aim to archive the deployment of students' skills.

The thing that has surprised me most is the students' or teachers' use of e-learning. An e-learning platform has been available in the college since a long time ago, and all lecturers are advised to use e-learning; they must all upload their course materials and assessments on the platform, and it is a compulsory policy. The fact is, though, that some teachers have not adopted e-learning, and some students do not use it.

Collections of personal stories in education

Besides my academic duty as an IT lecturer, I also held the highest position in Student Affairs Deanship in the college. This role addressed the concerns and issues of students in various areas. For instance, on a frequent basis, I had received students who had comments or questions about e-learning and its uses. Some of these concerns are explained in the examples and conversations described below:

- A student might come and say, "My final exam is done, and till today I haven't received my coursework mark, which is out of 50". My answer would be that "such marks are available on the e-learning web page". Then, the reply from the student would be "I don't use e-learning services. I'm not an IT student, so I don't know how to use it properly, and I don't have time to check it". *From this example, it can be seen that the student has an issue in using technological tools, such that he/she has no initiative in self-learning, and the student cannot manage his/her time.*

- Another student might show up with the difficulty of not being able to catch up with the course lecturer or other classmates, and he/she might have concerns about some points related to the course. Then, I would ask the student, "Did you try to put your concerns on the chat or discussion board of the same course on E-learning?" The answer in most cases would be the same as in the previous example, plus some students might give these answers: "I did not know that there was a chat or discussion group on there"; "I didn't think about that option"; "I am waiting for the technician or my classmate to set aside time to teach me how to use the group chat"; or "The course lecturer did not teach us how to use it". There might also be some pleasant responses, such as, "I have done that already, a long time ago, but nobody answered me." *This example shows issues with communication, independence, and technology use.*

- A student might have difficulty to meet the course teacher for example sometimes during his/her office hours, and will keep calling his/her office number, but the lecturer might not respond. I would advise the student to drop the teacher an email using the official college email address. Most of the replies from the students will be as follows: "I'm not using my college email"; "I use the e-learning portal and I sent the lecturer a private message, but I did not get any reply"; or the student might ask why the college has not linked the email into the e-learning page. *Here it can be seen that the student is ready to use email if it is linked to the E-learning system, and the course will add more advantages such as improving communication skills and keeping official records through the use of official accounts.*

- As an IT lecturer, I taught one of the courses that enrolled students from different undergraduate levels. The course delivery plan included a part related to graduate attributes (GAs), which illustrated the expected skills, and as a teacher,

I must explain GAs to the students at the beginning of the term. When I asked the students whether they were aware of GAs, I always got surprising answers. For example, few of the students said that they know about it and the majority of then said they didn not know anything about it - and that it is not important. *Because of this, I believe that there is a huge gap in the awareness of the GAs, as the students are less concerned about them, and if they understand that this part is very important, then it enables them to find out the important skills which they need to improve their future work, they would give it more attention and would try to meet the Gas. Here, a part of this concern is related to a lack of awareness and dependency skills.*

- As an IT teacher, when announcing a deadline on the e-learning portal for certain tasks, students would ask for extra time, because they have been unable to complete the tasks, and they have a lot of other tasks to complete at the same time. *This indicates a time management problem on the student part again.*

- When I enter a class, sometimes a conversation would take place along the following lines: a student would say, "I've sent you a question via WhatsApp, but I haven't got any text back". I would reply something like, "If you have any questions about the course, I would prefer you to send me an email, or an e-learning message". The reply from the student would be: "I don't even know what my college email account is, I've never used it, and I hardly use the e-learning platform". *This shows a lack of communication skills and commitment from the students.*

Conclusion

Most of the conversations above highlighted in one way or another that there is a gap in students' skills related to e-learning and some students lack some of the skills such as communication, time management, self-learning, ability to work under pressure, teamwork, independence and computing use. And, based on my own work experience, I realise that certain advantages can be emphasised by supporting and using e-learning; these advantages refer to students' and graduates' skills. Therefore, I use this to develop a study which will investigate how e-learning can make the students skilful in such competencies such as computing, English writing, communication, teamwork, time management and work under pressure.

Mohamad Adning

Mohamad Adning is Doctoral Researcher at Brunel University London. The Center for Information and Communication Technology Education and Culture, Ministry of Education and Culture, Republic of Indonesia sent him to improve his level of education in the field of education, particularly in the field of education technology. The majority of his academic work and research are focused on instructional design and educational technology. Nowadays, he is researching about continuing professional development for teachers through mobile phones.

Can the augmented reality and virtual reality be applied in the open university?

Mohamad Adning

Indonesia's Open University (Universitas Terbuka) has the biggest number of students in Indonesia. Universitas Terbuka (UT) was the 45th state university that was established in 1984 (Open University, 2020). Universitas Terbuka is the initiator of open and distance learning systems to serve all of its students. Universitas Terbuka offers 4 faculties with 33 study programmes, 6 master's programmes which offer a flexible and inexpensive university focusing on serving people who lack the opportunity to attend face-to-face mode of the higher education system (Open University, 2020). Consequently, the variety of age is vast, and the UT system should evolve and improve in terms of its teaching, learning systems, management, and to support services for students in many aspects.

I know quite well about the open and distance learning system while studying Educational Technology in my undergraduate and my master's degree. The opportunity to know more about open and distance learning systems became grew when I started working in 2005, at the Center for Information and Communication Technology Education and Culture, Ministry of Education and Culture, Republic of Indonesia (PUSTEKKOM, MoEC RI) which is now transforming into a Data and Information Technology Center (PUSDATIN, MoEC RI). One project in which I've been involved was the development of open learning for secondary school in Indonesia (SMA Terbuka). In Addition, PUSTEKKOM at that time developed many education technology systems, media and material to support learning process for any circumstances, such as distance learning systems and conventional methods. Those various opportunities finally gave me a comprehensive understanding of how to design learning for various levels and types of education.

One of services in cooperation between PUSTEKKOM and UT is the use of TV Edukasi (educational television owned by PUSTEKKOM, MoEC RI) as a medium to support learning process for UT's students throughout Indonesia. TV Edukasi broadcasts various UT content, which supports the learning process of students and was carried out in 2009-2011. Once again, I had the opportunity to become a member of the video content development team to support this. Besides, in an online tutorial at the Faculty of Education and Teacher Training (FKIP) UT, I am also involved as an outside lecturer who manages several modules. My involvement in various collaborative projects between UT and PUSTEKKOM strengthened my proficiency and personal experience as an instructional designer.

During the term of my research break (December 2019), UT challenged me to lead the project of developing media for learning based on contemporary technology, popularly known as augmented reality (AR) and virtual reality (VR) for undergraduate study programmes majoring in Education Technology. Most millennials recently know this technology (AR and VR) and access it by using a mobile phone. In addition, AR and VR are more familiar to games - and some sectors that use virtual reality to promote their products, such as the housing property industry. In the education field, AR and VR are recognised as learning sources to introduce difficult ideas and create interest in subjects. Some studies show that both have unique features and give lecturers, teachers and students a lot of new opportunities to improve learning outcomes and raising motivation (Erbas & Atherton, 2020; Mano, 2019). Aware of the extraordinary potentials owned by AR and VR, PUSTEKKOM and various institutions that relate to the field of education - and other fields - also produce a variety of content, both for the purposes of promotion, entertainment, and even learning. Rumah Belajar (an open resource educational portal developed by PUSTEKKOM that facilitates students, teachers and society with various learning resource) accommodates AR technology trends by developing AR-based learning content.

The potential of AR and VR as learning resources that provide a more tangible, and certainly "different", learning experience is also captured by UT as a higher education institution that must always innovate in optimising the use of ICT to support their learning systems. Diverse student characteristics, learning approaches that are also different from other universities in general are a challenge for UT to provide the best service, including providing a variety of learning resources that can enrich the student's learning experience. The concepts of open education and learning independence as main characteristics of learning process at UT are accommodated in online tutorials. In addition, the system that developed should be incorporated into the Moodle platform that they have in an online tutorial at the Faculty of Education and Teacher Training (FKIP) UT (figure 1).

The voice of educators and education students

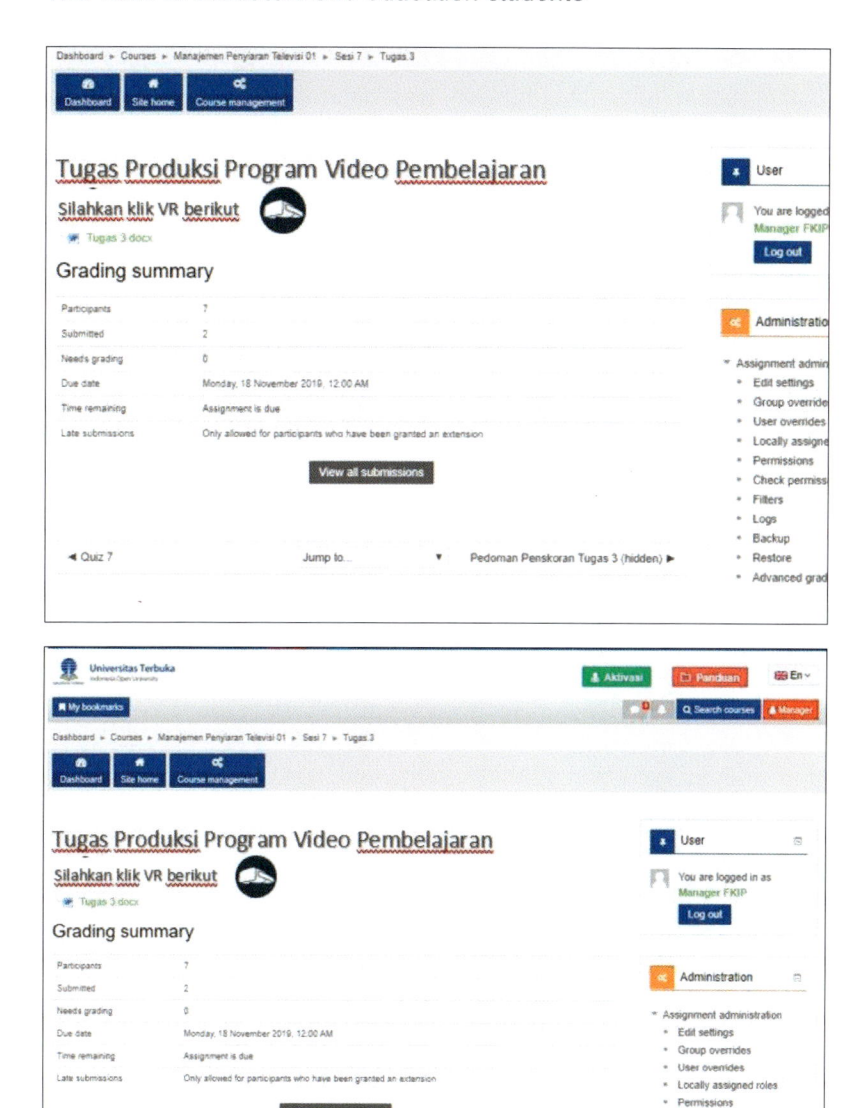

Figure 1. Configuration of AR and VR in the e-learning system UT

So, I was trusted to design and develop AR and VR-based content that was built into a comprehensive system and integrated with UT's online tutorials. Together with the teams from UT and

PUSDATIN, we collaborated in all stages of its development (analysis, design, develompent, implementation, and evaluation/ ADDIE). Teams must consider minimum mobile phone specifications and entry-level behaviour for students using these apps, etc. Furthermore, micro-learning, guideline instruction should be clearly provided to support this system, as students operate on their own without a lecturer, and they learn by themselves or self-study using an online system.

In developing this project and to make it work, I must elaborate and lead many experts not only instructional design, lecturer but also the AR and VR programmers. Approximately 20 people were involved in this project, but most by the two official government services (UT and PUSDATIN, MoEC), that sent people with different backgrounds and education to support the project. PUSDATIN assigned 8 instructional designers who have backgrounds and experiences in television broadcasting and multimedia system, while UT assigned 3 instructional designers (from Central Multimedia Development, UT) and 3 lectures from Educational Technology programmes. The rest are AR and VR programmers.

Figure 2. Half of the AR and VR Team Members (UT and PUSDATIN)

In a short time, teams began to analyse 12 modules that are likely to be developed by AR and VR. Three experts (material expert, media expert and stakeholder) were involved in the discussion. All of the team members must be firm that the AR and VR that they develop shows the real thing and offers an interesting learning experience for the students. As an initial stage, teams decided to develop AR and VR to complement the online modules, namely Management of Broadcasting and Video Production. Both modules are fundamental because they are related to knowledge and skills needed in broadcasting systems. AR and VR must show the real conditions of in-studio TV, real equipment, the holistic process in producing video/tv programmes and broadcasting processes. Based on our need assessment from 2 modules, we will develop 4 VR content related to broadcast management, with topics such as: job description of production crew, Master Control Room system, Format and Genre in TV programming. Meanwhile, the Video Production module incorporates 4 AR topics (camera, tripod, lighting, and audio equipment) and 1 VR, about Video Production.

The deadline for this project has been set by the Dean of the Faculty of Education and Teacher Training (FKIP) UT. They are giving the timeline to implement on academic calendar 2019/2020 (March-May 2020). I have been planning for these programmes to be developed for six months. We choose ADDIE (analyses, design, development, implements and evaluation) as generic model for developing the AR and VR. I made a plan and schedule for finishing every step of the model. I separated these into three steps, first analyses, design as a one-step early on in December 2019. The second step is the development of AR and VR, including scripts, storyboards and programmes (January-February 2020). Step three will implement AR and VR in April until May 2020, and the final step will be the evaluation in May 2020. We believe that this project is a pilot project for a number of future projects. While I am writing this paper, the project will continue to make progress until July 2020.

In each stage carried out during this project, my team and I hope to get an understanding of best practice and of how AR and VR can become learning media that have a strategic role in realising a multi-source based learning process. AR and VR hope to be in line with the concept of freedom in learning that allows students to choose topics and learn as needed, anywhere, anytime.

References

Erbas, C. and Atherton, S. (2020) 'A content analysis of augmented reality studies published in 2017', *Journal of Learning and Teaching in Digital Age*, 5(1), pp. 7-15.

Mano, R. M. C. (2019) *The benefits of virtual reality in education.* Available at: https://blend.media/blog/benefits-of-360-videos-virtual-reality-in-education.

Open University (2020) *Brief history Indonesia open university.* Avaialbe at: https://www.ut.ac.id/en/brief-history (Accessed: 8 February 2020).

The voice of educators and education students

Lisa Arthur Bonful

Me Firi Ghana (I come from Ghana) and I am studying Masters of Arts Education (Professional Practice and Pedagogy) at Brunel University. I am a housing professional, with many year's experiences dealing with all walks of life. My interest in Education stemmed from wanting to help individuals to have a better learning experience. I believe that 'knowledge is power' which is why I enjoy studying/ teaching in and out of university.

Online student tutoring from a tutor's perspective

Lisa Arthur Bonful

Online tutoring: what is the appeal? My passion for tutoring began when I excelled in my assignments and other students approached me for assistance with their assignments. I gladly accepted and quickly assumed the role as a tutor, breaking down questions for them to understand and develop a tailored student learning plan. My excitement grew as my students informed me about their good grades they received and I realised that tutoring is something that I would like to incorporate in my everyday life. Research has shown that nearly one in four young people in the UK have received private or home tuition from tutoring agencies. Online tutoring has grown as a sector, with an online tutoring service called MyTutorWeb, which has enabled 3,500 tutoring sessions, delivered by Oxbridge and Russell Group university students at £17 an hour. On most days the website signs up six new parents in search of tutors. Enhancements in technology and broadband over recent years has enabled the ability to offer high-quality one-to-one teaching for children at an affordable price (Telegraph Media Group Limited, 2020). According to Guill et al., (2019) tutoring has always been an important part of education and schooling. Private tutoring refers to tutoring in academic subjects for example languages, mathematics, or science) with the aim of improving academic achievement. It is provided by tutors for financial gain and does not exclude extracurricular activities, such as sports or musical activities. Tutoring can be effective as it gives students more time to learn, provides the opportunity for tutors to expand and consolidate material covered in school lessons. The benefits of tutoring are that it can occur in a face-to-face setting or online which enables the learning experience to take place. This contribution will discuss my personal experiences as an online tutor and the benefits it brings to myself and my students.

Starting my journey as an online tutor was a new experience and the nervous feeling of not succeeding often crossed my mind. I overcame this feeling eventually as my students were highly engaged which in turn made me feel valued. Online tutoring is very rewarding, it provides the ability to conduct lessons within my home environment, without having to be in place of work or be stuck in traffic trying to get to the location for the lesson. The majority of participants in O'Hare's (2011) study highlighted 'how they watched how students grow and develop over a study period' and 'they were surprised with the relationships they had built with their students'. Similarly, I have built strong relationships with my students, where they are able to express their views freely and this has contributed to their growth in learning. Other features of online tutoring that appealed to me is that it allowed me to be involved in teaching, without experiencing the issues faced in a classroom environment. Online tutoring will also help me to develop a career in education, a career which helps transforms students' educational experiences. However, although online tutoring has its appeal there are some challenges that I come across in my tutoring, such as maintaining a work-life balance. Time management becomes a crucial skill that I have to adopt in order to manage my time effectively and ensure that I set time aside specifically for tutoring.

A typical tutoring lesson starts off with a general conversation with the student, creating that friendly atmosphere whilst maintaining the professional boundary of a student and tutor relationship. This breaks the ice and allows for the lesson to run smoothly for both student and tutor. The lesson begins with objectives, a fun Youtube video to engage the mind, then swiftly moving on to worksheets for my student to work on whilst I countdown time, waiting patiently for my student to answer the questions. My lesson revolves around allowing my students to use their mind to answer questions set, to enable them to fully understand the topic. It usually ends with a summary of the lesson and what the student has learnt from the lesson. The tutoring cycle continues in this sequence.

Online tutoring has as much influence as face-to-face tutoring, in shaping the learning environment and outcomes for the student. It carries the responsibility for creating conditions that encourages a deep approach to learning, which demonstrates a dynamic and interactive community. As O'Hare (2011) highlights that from a teacher's perspective, online tutoring requires having pedagogical skills and content knowledge that allows them to manage a learning environment that develops and encourages students to think critically and to learn independently. She further adds that from each student's perspective, this requires a higher-order cognitive processing that includes critical thinking and self-direction. Virtual classrooms replicate real classrooms typically allowing students and tutors to talk, share files, draw diagrams and send messages. This allows the tutoring experience to be just as effective. I particularly enjoy the virtual classroom as it provides the opportunity to be creative and really engage in an interactive learning session with my students. I find that it encourages my students to think and engage more in the learning activities. Online tutoring allows you to put a face to the name with the use of webcam and this allows the environment to duplicate a real-life classroom, which makes the experience exciting.

I believe online tutoring is the way forward as it convinces both student and tutor, and can be done anywhere and anytime. I enjoy tutoring as it is an extension of the real-life classroom and allows for a deeper level of learning to take place. I continue to be appealed by tutoring due to gaining satisfaction from helping students to improve their grades, building short or long term relationships, developing tailored learning plans and just genuinely wanting to make a positive difference to my student's lives. Online Tutoring is definitely an area that I would like to expand and grow in the future and transform student's learning experiences.

References

Guill, K., Ludtke, O and Koller, O. (2019) 'Assessing the instructional quality of private tutoring and its effects on student outcomes: analyses from the German national educational panel study', *British Journal of Educational Psychology,* pp. 1-19. doi:10.1111/bjep.12281.

O'Hare, S. (2011) 'The role of the tutor in online learning', in G. Williams, P. Statham, N. Brown and B. Cleland (eds.) *Changing Demands, Changing Directions, Proceedings ascilite Hobart*, Australia, pp. 909- 918.

Telegraph Media Group Limited (2020) *Online tutoring is the safe, convenient way for your child to learn.* Available at: https://www.telegraph.co.uk/education-and-careers/2020/03/23/tutors-becoming-popular-knowits-time-get-one-child/ (Accessed: 16 March 2020).

Printed in Great Britain
by Amazon